Comfort
FOR
TIMES
of LOSS

Praying
for you
Mrs Lewis

Love;
Kimberly
Richardson
from next
door

ISBN 978-1-64352-222-7

Published by Barbour Books, an imprint of Barbour Publishing, Inc., 1810 Barbour Drive, Uhrichsville, Ohio 44683, www.barbourbooks.com

Our mission is to inspire the world with the life-changing message of the Bible.

Member of the
Evangelical Christian
Publishers Association

Comfort FOR TIMES of LOSS

90 Devotions for a Grieving Heart

Anita Higman

BARBOUR BOOKS
An Imprint of Barbour Publishing, Inc.

INTRODUCTION

In this life, if you come to love someone—then at some point you will endure heartache and grief. There is both beauty and peril in loving. *Comfort for Times of Loss* is not a book from a clinical perspective, but instead, it is a gathering of hope-filled meditations that follow some of the stages of grieving with their unpredictable ebb and flow. These ninety devotions are written by a fellow sojourner who has experienced loss and grief and who has discovered that no matter how harsh this earthly landscape can be at times, we do not walk it alone. . . .

A GENTLE SLUMBER

He lets me lie down in green pastures;
He leads me beside the still and quiet waters.
He refreshes and restores my soul (life).
PSALM 23:2–3 AMP

That favorite stream of yours meanders through the valley with such tranquility, you're always compelled to follow it. To listen to the gurgling sounds of the water as it makes its way across the stones. Perhaps you find a golden spot in a nearby meadow and you choose to nap in the grasses.

The world doesn't quite understand the value of those quiet moments when you're grieving over a loved one's passing. Humanity continues to whirl on at a feverish pace as if completely callous to your plight. That fact can be painful and confusing and even infuriating. You may want to scream at the world, "How dare you laugh and joke and carry on as if life is wonderful."

While the world is swirling on without you, you don't have to succumb to the pressure of joining in. If you need some quiet time and extra rest, that is good. If you feel up to joining in with friends and family or talking about your pain, then do so. But don't let people convince you that you must hurry the process of grieving.

This is a time for the Almighty's gift of rest. Yes, it is time for the nourishment of doing nothing for a while and the sustenance of surrendering to God's restful ways. Give yourself plenty of time for the Lord's green pastures and His quiet waters. In doing so, Jesus promises to restore your soul.

Lord, I am bone tired and soul weary, trying to cope with my shock wave of grief. I need some rest. Please show me how to quiet my mind so I can sleep. Amen.

YOUR HEARTS WILL REJOICE

———◆———

"Truly, truly, I say to you, you will weep and lament, but the world will rejoice. You will be sorrowful, but your sorrow will turn into joy. When a woman is giving birth, she has sorrow because her hour has come, but when she has delivered the baby, she no longer remembers the anguish, for joy that a human being has been born into the world. So also you have sorrow now, but I will see you again, and your hearts will rejoice, and no one will take your joy from you."
JOHN 16:20–22 ESV

*S*teve had it all—great Christian wife, kids, job, house, everything he had hoped for in life. And then his wife died suddenly of a heart attack. One moment she was there, vibrant and healthy and loving life. And then she was in the hospital emergency room, surrounded by machines and doctors trying to save her. But they couldn't. His wife was gone, and the sudden severing of that close relationship, that love, wasn't going to be bearable as far as he could see. He was suffering. His kids were suffering. The shock of it had not worn off, and the hospital scenes played in his head over and over and over.

Out in the garage, Steve tried to work on his car, but it was no use. He wiped the sweat from his brow and then let the hood slam down. All at once, he wondered what his wife was doing right then in heaven. Something joyful, no doubt. That part, that hope, did bring him peace, knowing where she was and knowing that in the Lord's timing, he too would know that same joy.

*Lord God, I am grateful for
the hope of heaven! Amen.*

THAT SACRED MOMENT

———— ✦ ————

Precious in the sight of the LORD
is the death of his faithful ones.
PSALM 116:15 NRSV

*Y*ou hold your dear grandmother's hand as she lies dying in the hospital bed. She had been a faithful follower of Christ, and her beloved hands show the wrinkles of holy use. They had been busy for a lifetime hugging, baking, cleaning, sharing, opening the pages of scripture, playing games, and doing all the many things that grandmothers do best. Oh, how you will miss seeing her face light up when you come into the room. How you will miss her wise words and quick wit.

Your grandmother's faint smile fades as she closes her eyes. You bring her soft hand to your cheek as your heart breaks into pieces. How will you bear her absence? You cry out to God, "Why must she go now? Couldn't we keep her awhile longer?"

These moments of loving and remembering and letting go are not taken lightly by our Lord. They are sacred moments. Psalms reminds us,

"Precious in the sight of the LORD is the death of his faithful ones." Know this truth down deep in your soul. Take comfort in the promise of it. Also know that when this cherished grandmother takes in her last breath on earth, she will then take in her first fragrant and freeing breath of heaven.

Father God, I don't want to let go of my loved one, and yet I know I must. Help me know that she is entering the gates of heaven to be with You forever. Please give me that peace and assurance that I will one day see her again. And in the meantime, let me rest in Your tender mercies and Your abundant love. In Jesus' name I pray. Amen.

WALKING WITH GOD

When you go through deep waters and great trouble,
I will be with you. When you go through rivers
of difficulty, you will not drown! When you walk
through the fire of oppression, you will not be
burned up—the flames will not consume you.

ISAIAH 43:2 TLB

*L*ife can indeed feel like we are drowning in rivers of difficulty. Or we are walking through the fires of oppression. We feel these emotions most agonizingly intense when someone we love dies. We didn't even know that we could hurt so much. That the feeling of loss in our hearts could be so shocking and ruthless.

Our spirits were not meant to go through the loss and grief we experience here on earth. We were created for paradise in the Garden of Eden. Beauty and bliss and walking with God in the cool of the evening—that is how life was meant to be. But in this fallen world—this paradise lost— we have deep waters and great trouble. We have adversities we can't cope with and burdens we can't carry. But even in our rebellion, God made a way for us through Christ. And the Bible is filled with promises that God will watch over us. That these deep waters and great troubles will not overtake us if we cling to Him. The Lord alone can save us. Cling to Him.

Oh God, I feel that too many friends and family members are saying all the wrong things. Too many people are offering help and food and advice I do not need. What I need most is You, God, to rescue me from all the dark fears that threaten to consume me. Please come now and take my hand. In Jesus' powerful name I pray. Amen.

TANGLED THOUGHTS

———◆———

"So do not fear, for I am with you;
do not be dismayed, for I am your God.
I will strengthen you and help you; I will
uphold you with my righteous right hand."
ISAIAH 41:10 NIV

*I*magine the darkest night. The deepest pit. The cruelest blow. This can describe the death of a cherished spouse.

You can feel the sorrow that death brings, and you can even describe its sharp and fearsome talons in your heart, and yet something in you still wants to deny the passing of your spouse. It cannot be—you do not want it to be! You're desperate to imagine that your husband will pull up in the driveway or call suddenly from work or saunter into the kitchen for a cup of coffee as always. Why couldn't his death have been no more than a terrible nightmare and you could simply wake up? Tangled thoughts force their way into your head. *Why did it have to happen to my husband? Why now? Did God really allow it? What will I do with all my years to come? I feel fear and dread all around me, Lord.*

The Bible has wisdom for us in times of grief. Do not allow fear to overtake you. You do not need to despair. God is with you. He will help you, strengthen you. The Lord will uphold you with His righteous hand.

Dearest Lord, I still can't believe my loved one is gone. I'm struggling, trying to deal with the shock, the anxiety and the lonesomeness of this news. Please let Your promises sink deeply into my soul. Let me not stay in that dark night and that deepest pit. Please uphold me with Your righteous hand! Amen.

WHEN LIFE IS TOO HARD

He will keep in perfect peace all those who trust in him, whose thoughts turn often to the Lord!
ISAIAH 26:3 TLB

*A*mid Gloria's mourning over the loss of her mother, she did get a little sleep. But once there in that safe cocoon, getting out of bed seemed to be a laborious task. People were busy calling. Life was moving but such a blur. Family members were asking questions. Too many questions. The words "Making arrangements for the funeral" hung in the air like a dark entity no one wanted to look at. And yet she was being forced to look at it, think about it, and decide a hundred things. What should they dress their mother in at the funeral home? What hymns should be played? What flowers chosen? Photos gathered? Food served? Did someone call all the relatives and friends? Could she write a eulogy?

Then in the middle of Gloria's battle for clarity, strength, and sanity, she released a laugh. She had no idea why. It didn't feel all that good, but it came out just the same. What was wrong?

Laughter seemed so inappropriate. Perhaps her mind wasn't functioning properly. She was obviously overwrought. She wished people around her would stop whispering behind her back. She wished a million things, but mostly she wished that her mother—her dearest friend—had not been taken.

Lord, why is life so hard and complicated? I know we live in a sinful and broken world, but why does living here need to be so very difficult? And yet. . . I am going to step out in faith and trust You, Lord. Please help me get through all that must be done, and keep me safe in Your perfect peace. Amen.

WHOSE HAND WILL I TAKE?

I think you ought to know, dear brothers,
about the hard time we went through in Asia.
We were really crushed and overwhelmed,
and feared we would never live through it. We
felt we were doomed to die and saw how powerless
we were to help ourselves; but that was good, for
then we put everything into the hands of God, who
alone could save us, for he can even raise the dead.
2 CORINTHIANS 1:8–9 TLB

This world is a dangerous place to live. As we can see in this passage in 2 Corinthians, living had reached a pinnacle of anguish and despair for the apostle Paul. He felt that the calamities he faced would kill him. But in the end, he persevered, trusting in God for his deliverance. Paul even felt that the suffering was good in that it caused him to put everything into the hands of God. Everything. Paul knew that only God could save, only God could raise the dead. Paul knew.

Whom do you choose to trust when someone dies? When your world falls apart and you feel utterly alone? When you feel powerless to change a thing? Whom do you trust when the enemy torments you with fears in the night? Whom do you turn to when loneliness and depression chase you relentlessly? Whom do you run to when you've come to the end of all your hopes—to the end of yourself?

Whose hand do you reach out to?

Almighty God, I too have been crushed by this life. I too am overwhelmed. I feel as though I will never survive this calamity. But even then, in my despair, just like Paul, I choose You. In Jesus' name I pray. Amen.

A TIME TO MOURN

A time to weep and a time to laugh;
a time to mourn and a time to dance.
ECCLESIASTES 3:4 AMP

If you come across a stranger who's crying, you might feel bewildered. Right away you wonder what happened. You're wishing you could help. Or maybe you feel awkward or hesitant. You might think, *Do I stop to offer help or a listening ear? Should I give her a hug? A word of encouragement? Maybe she just wants to be left alone.*

Even if the person is your best friend, it's hard to know how to handle tears. People tend to be private with their emotions, so we become almost incapacitated when we actually see someone sobbing or tearful. But we can overcome the need to flee from those who grieve as well as the need to hold back our own emotions when the time comes to weep. After all, God gave us tear ducts for a reason. We can use them.

Crying because we will miss someone we've loved is not a sin. In fact, the book of Ecclesiastes reminds us that there is a time for weeping and a time for mourning. If you are grieving, it means you cared for someone dearly. It means you risked your heart in a big way. Sorrow may be the price to be paid for such love, but love is right and good. Yes, there is a season for everything under heaven, including a time to weep. Remember, though, that the Lord remains with you, and His tears mingle with yours.

Dearest Lord, I am afraid that if I start crying I will never be able to stop. Help me be able to express my sorrow and shed my tears in a healthy way. Amen.

EVEN IN THE
THROES OF GRIEF

*Carry one another's burdens and in this way
you will fulfill the requirements of the law
of Christ [that is, the law of Christian love].*
GALATIANS 6:2 AMP

While your heart is mending and you're resting on the couch, a dear friend quietly brings you a soft pillow and a comfy blanket. The friend arrived with no chatter, no questions, and she expected no gushing thanks. She came with a servant's heart and a willingness to carry your burden with you—even if few words pass between you. Your friend gingerly tucks you in and then leaves a pot of tea and a snack on the coffee table. Your grief has made you forget your appetite, and you have no desire for tea, but the act of kindness warms your heart. And the scent of the tea makes you think of God.

Yes, God is still there, even though the days of mourning seem almost unbearable. He is there. Even in this ominous storm you can see the faintest light. You can sense that He is speaking kind and soothing words to you. And you see the goodness of God as people—those blessed earthly angels—gently take care of you. Love you. Help you. Yes, God is there, and His helpers are there too. Even in the throes of grief and sorrow, yes, God is good. He will provide.

Heavenly Father, I so appreciate Your earthly angels who have a big heart for mankind. They don't need a lot of attention or explanations or constant compliments. They just want to be Your servants in a time of mourning. Thank You for these folks who are such a precious gift from Your hand. In Jesus' name I pray. Amen.

WAKING UP WITH TEARS

———————— ••• ————————

*"And I will ask the Father, and He will give
you another Helper (Comforter, Advocate,
Intercessor—Counselor, Strengthener, Standby),
to be with you forever—the Spirit of Truth,
whom the world cannot receive [and take to its
heart] because it does not see Him or know Him,
but you know Him because He (the Holy Spirit)
remains with you continually and will be in you."*
JOHN 14:16–17 AMP

*Y*ou wake up with your hands tearing at the sheets. Sweat trickles off your forehead as your heart races. What a terrible dream! A mountain lion had been chasing you, and the beast had nearly captured you in its powerful claws. "Only a nightmare," you whisper as you reach out to your sleeping husband for comfort.

Then all the real horror comes flooding in— the living nightmare that you had forgotten in your sleep. Your husband is no longer there. He's gone to heaven without you. Despair is now chasing you, wanting to consume you in that dark night. Hopelessness tears at your spirit. Tears drizzle down onto your pillow. You cry out to the Lord to send His Comforter. "Please God! Help me!"

We see in the book of John that the Holy Spirit is a Comforter, Advocate, Intercessor, Counselor, Strengthener, and Standby. There is great hope in that passage, and a supernatural blessing. The Lord will not leave you comfortless in your time of need. Trust in His everlasting love and His promises.

Lord Jesus, I am frightened and all alone. Fears of all kinds are chasing me. Please send the Comforter, Your Holy Spirit, to help me in my time of need. May He calm my racing heart, support my failing strength, and bring me back to a place of peace and rest. Amen.

STAGGERING UNDER
THE WEIGHT

———————— ◆ ————————

"It is the LORD who goes before you.
He will be with you; he will not leave you
or forsake you. Do not fear or be dismayed."
DEUTERONOMY 31:8 ESV

$\mathcal{W}$hat happens when life does its worst to you—when you are faced with the death of your beloved? The shock of it may make you feel paralyzed with an unfamiliar emptiness or a strange numbness. Perhaps you can barely speak, or instead, you unexpectedly lash out at a friend. You might shout at the heavens in utter fear and helplessness. You worry that you might collapse or that you're teetering on the edge of a mental breakdown.

Each person will experience those first days of devastating loss in his or her own way—especially if it happens suddenly—and people may react in ways that are very unpredictable.

In the jolting alarm of tragic news, reach out to the Lord. Jesus experienced grief firsthand, whether it came from the death of a close friend or through the knowledge that He was about to hang on a cross for the sins of mankind. He knew well the pain of living here on this fallen earth. And He knows how you feel this very minute. But there is so much more to Jesus than His "knowing." He is about caring and comforting too. He will be with you. He promises never to leave you. Never to forsake you. Christ is right here, right now. Reach out to Him.

Lord, I am in shock and can barely breathe. Please lessen the weight of my suffering, for I am staggering under its burden. Hold me fast, Mighty God. I am in desperate need of Your gentle words and tender care. In Jesus' powerful name I pray. Amen.

HOPE STIRRED

Your word is a lamp for my feet,
a light on my path.
PSALM 119:105 NIV

*B*everly sat on the chair staring out the front window of her home. She noticed a little boy riding his tricycle up the sidewalk with his mom hovering close behind. The mother was so affectionate toward her child and the woman looked so happy, tears welled up in Beverly's eyes as they did so often now. The tricycle scene was one of many she had played in her mind as she excitedly waited for her first child. But it was not meant to be.

People had used the word *miscarriage* when they talked about her tiny baby boy. Such an emotionless word connected to such love. Beverly wanted to shout at the world, "This was a life!" A beautiful child. *Her* child. He had a name— Phillip. Now he was God's child. But then, of course, tiny Phillip had always been God's child too, and in His capable hands, she would have to leave him.

She still wondered, though, about a thousand motherhood moments—moments that could have been. Beverly placed her hands against her empty womb. What would the future bring? Was there hope buried somewhere in her sorrow? Right now, her existence felt lightless, her soul cold. She didn't even want to get out of the chair, let alone move on with life. And yet even in the despair, hope stirred.

Oh Lord, I have felt as though I'm fading away. That I have been lost in a dark and scary place. But for the first time, I feel a tiny stirring of hope for the future. I believe that is You coming to rescue me. Please, Lord, I really need Your light. May Your Word illuminate my life path. Amen.

THOSE SACRED TEARS

———— •• ————

Rejoice with those who rejoice [sharing others' joy],
and weep with those who weep [sharing others' grief].
ROMANS 12:15 AMP

*H*ave you ever been suffering with sorrow—
so much so that your emotions were hanging by
a thread? Sometimes friends can be a great help
in times of mourning and can lift you back up to
safety. At other times friends can add extra tension
to that already strained emotional cord.

Julie had just lost her best friend since high
school. They had stayed close for thirty years, and
when that same friend died, Julie felt devastated.
One day when she was at home grieving, a group
of her workout buddies arrived with a bag of
healthy muffins and a plan to make Julie shorten
her bereavement. The batch of five ladies coun-
seled, chided, preached, cajoled, joked, chattered,
chortled, pontificated, and judged, and when that
didn't work, they began to bully. Finally, after
Julie burst into tears, she kindly asked her friends
to leave.

The next day when another friend showed up,

Julie almost didn't answer the door. But when Julie did sit down to tea with her friend, the woman said little. Mostly, she listened. Finally Julie felt safe enough to open up more, and she shared her story, her heart, and her tears. The friend sat and wept with her, and in that holy hush of sacred tears, Julie felt some solace and even some lightening of the heart.

Perhaps humanity's sea of good intentions can get swept away too easily by insensitivity. But when mourners find a real friend, they are given the love and heart of Christ.

Lord, I thank You for friends who are compassionate listeners and who weep with me when the burden becomes too heavy. Amen.

YOUR BEAUTIFUL WORD

———— •◆• ————

*Even when walking through the dark valley of
death I will not be afraid, for you are close
beside me, guarding, guiding all the way.*
PSALM 23:4 TLB

$\mathcal{I}$magine you're standing in the middle of a
great salt plain at dusk and you're all alone. There
before you is a landscape of white salt for as far
as the eye can see. Darkness is fast approaching,
the winds are howling, and eerie shadows seem to
stalk you. What a bleak and lonely experience! If
you couldn't get in your car and drive away, you
might feel abandoned and desperate.

When we're faced with the death of someone
we love greatly, it feels as though we'll never escape
those fearsome and desolate feelings. In fact, they
can take over every part of our lives—every wak-
ing thought and every sleepless night. The torment
can permeate our very souls.

There are many places in the Bible that
speak directly to these harsh life journeys. These
scriptures calm us, support us, and bring us peace
and hope. Allow the Holy Spirit to use these sweet

and holy words from Psalm 23:4 to permeate your spirit and remind you that God is real and reliable. He is caring and tender. He is mighty and eternal.

Take heart, and know that the Lord will love you through the deepest valleys and the darkest hours. "Even when walking through the dark valley of death I will not be afraid, for you are close beside me, guarding, guiding all the way."

Almighty God, I am in a desolate place right now. I need Your beautiful and promising words to inspire me and lift me up. I need You by my side, guarding me and guiding me. I will put my trust in You. Amen.

THE ANGER RISING

*So to keep me from becoming conceited because of the
surpassing greatness of the revelations, a thorn was
given me in the flesh, a messenger of Satan to harass
me, to keep me from becoming conceited. Three times
I pleaded with the Lord about this, that it should leave
me. But he said to me, "My grace is sufficient for you,
for my power is made perfect in weakness." Therefore
I will boast all the more gladly of my weaknesses,
so that the power of Christ may rest upon me.*

2 CORINTHIANS 12:7–9 ESV

Of all the emotions Jane experienced after the
death of her dad, she didn't quite know what to
do with her rising anger. She couldn't understand
why God hadn't allowed him to stay longer—
or even a little longer. Surely his healing wouldn't
have messed up any grand earthly plan. Her
dad had been her friend and confidant since her
mom had died. The heartache now felt double. She
had made so many cries to heaven. Why had her
heartfelt prayers not been answered? She sighed.

Then Jane remembered the verse in 2 Corinthians where Paul talked about his thorn in the

flesh. Paul had asked the Lord three times for this harassment to be taken away, and yet God chose not to remove it. Many times, Jane had asked for her father to be healed, and yet God chose not to heal him. God surely had another plan. Jane came to know that Christ's grace was indeed sufficient, not just for others, but for her too.

Lord, like most people, I am the kind of person who likes to know the whys behind everything. But I know that in Your plan I may not understand all things on this side of eternity. So, I will choose to have faith instead. Amen.

WHEN PATIENCE RUNS THIN

———————•———————

But the fruit of the Spirit is love, joy, peace,
forbearance, kindness, goodness, faithfulness, gentleness
and self-control. Against such things there is no law.
GALATIANS 5:22–23 NIV

*A*fter the death of a loved one, patience can sometimes run a little thin. Relatives and friends can sometimes get on your nerves, especially if they're staying in your home during and after a funeral. Some neighbors or coworkers with good intentions may say all the wrong things.

Then there are the folks who are "controllers." They tend to come out of the woodwork when they see someone who is vulnerable. And when you're going through the passages of grief, it is easy to appear helpless. The mourner can unknowingly leave herself open to a controller. These individuals may want to help decide all the elements of the funeral for you. They may want to give you spiritual advice, financial advice, and health advice. They may even want to tell you who your friends should be. What you should eat and drink. What you need to do about the future. What you should think and feel. How you need to "move on" from your grief. You get the picture. Yes, praying for patience is biblical and good, but people who are grieving are not obligated to keep a controller hovering around. God may tell you to gently and lovingly bow out of any friendships that add conflict, confusion, or anxiousness to your already grief-laden condition. Ask God to provide you with friends who are good at listening and encouraging and loving instead.

Lord, I am in the midst of sorrow, and some of my family and friends are adding to my misery. As I grieve, please help me have discernment and wisdom in all my relationships. Amen.

A GENTLE WHISPER

"Go out and stand before me on the mountain," the Lord told him. And as Elijah stood there the Lord passed by, and a mighty windstorm hit the mountain; it was such a terrible blast that the rocks were torn loose, but the Lord was not in the wind. After the wind, there was an earthquake, but the Lord was not in the earthquake. And after the earthquake, there was a fire, but the Lord was not in the fire. And after the fire, there was the sound of a gentle whisper.

1 KINGS 19:11–12 TLB

George and his wife had always loved a good baseball game. It was one of the greatest joys for them both—to sit together eating popcorn and cheering for their favorite team. But George was alone now, ever since his beloved wife had passed on to heaven. He no longer found joy in watching a game, so he sat quietly on the couch. He had no idea what the future might look like. He was truly alone now, except for some anger. Even though he tried not to admit it to his friends or his pastor or even himself, he was mad at God. He wasn't sure what to do with the feeling. No one had the right to be angry with God, right? God was holy and good and without blame. So, where could this firestorm of anger flow? What could he do now, after such an earthquake-like shock of loss?

Then in the quiet of the living room, he sensed something—Someone. Even in his anger, God was still there. Even then. And so, George poured out his heart.

Lord, please release me from this anger
and comfort me in my profound loss. Amen.

NEAR TO THE
BROKENHEARTED

———————◆———————

*The LORD is near to the brokenhearted, and saves
the crushed in spirit. Many are the afflictions of the
righteous, but the LORD rescues them from them all.*
PSALM 34:18–19 NRSV

A delicate crystal vase fell over and shattered
into a hundred pieces. Iris didn't care. In fact,
she may have not so accidentally knocked it off
the table. Maybe she wanted to see something
more broken than she was. Maybe it made her
feel less alone.

She had wanted and needed to cry after the
funeral of her dear little sister, Lou, but the tears
would not come even when she willed them to.
Then when Iris hit her toe on the leg of the coffee
table, the tears flowed out in rivers. Perhaps Iris
had been afraid that if she started to weep she
would never stop. Losing her best friend in the
world—her sister—had been much harder than
she ever imagined. Oh, how she had loved her. Still
did. They had known the details of each other's

moods and foibles and strong points. They had loved each other no matter the trials or seasons. They understood each other and made each other's lives better and happier just by being there. Now little Lou was gone. Life felt all wrong and upside down without her. Iris bowed her head. She cried out to the Lord, for she still believed that He was her help in times of trouble.

Lord, You know how heart-close I was to my loved one. I miss her more than I can even express right now. Could You please be near me, for I am truly brokenhearted. I need Your loving hand to rescue me from my bewilderment and sadness and emptiness. Amen.

TOO MANY EMOTIONS

*"I am the LORD, the God of all mankind.
Is anything too hard for me?"*
JEREMIAH 32:27 NIV

*V*ictoria's emotions were all over the place. First, she felt merely numb and depressed over the death of her beloved aunt. But then the emotions swung over to a near panic attack from a sudden and intense wave of grief. It had started out innocently enough, in that Victoria saw her aunt's favorite tea—black currant. The beautiful canister made her think of the aroma, the taste, and the warmth of it. Then the sweet memories of her aunt came flooding back, along with their unique comradery and friendship. Sometimes it had almost seemed like they could converse without talking because they knew each other's heart and mind so well. She and her aunt could cry with each other and then laugh until they were nearly breathless. *What memories,* Victoria thought.

But just as soon as a wave of memories and grief was over, her emotions landed on another feeling. Since Victoria had helped with some of the caregiving for her aunt toward the last months of her life, she also felt twinges of relief. Not just that her aunt was not in pain anymore, but that she could now move on with her own life. But that sentiment felt like pure selfishness to Victoria. Whatever was going on, whether it was selfishness or not, Victoria knew she needed the Lord's help to sort out all her feelings. Because nothing, she knew, was too hard for the Almighty.

Lord, I am a mess of too many emotions right now. I am so confused about the myriad of thoughts I'm experiencing. Even in my grieving, may I continue to honor You. May the mediations of my heart always please You. Amen.

HIS MERCIES NEVER CEASE

I will never forget this awful time, as I grieve over
my loss. Yet I still dare to hope when I remember
this: The faithful love of the LORD never ends!
His mercies never cease. Great is his faithfulness;
his mercies begin afresh each morning.
LAMENTATIONS 3:20–23 NLT

*N*ot long after the funeral, Anna discovered some unfamiliar paperwork in her husband's desk, documents that she'd never seen before. In her research, she discovered that much of their retirement savings had been spent by her husband. She was now not too far from financial ruin. She might even lose the house that they had lived in all their married life. Anna thought, *Oh, if only he had handled our financial affairs properly, I wouldn't need to go back to work in my retirement years!* Her grief mixed itself with anger toward her husband. The concentrated brew of emotions was enough to make her sleepless and sick. Her friends tried to console her, her pastor attempted to encourage her, and her kids begged to help her. But she stayed at home weeping and angry until she couldn't even stand to be around herself anymore.

Finally, Anna knew what she had to do. Trust in God again. His faithful love would never end. His mercies would never cease. Yes, that is what she needed more than anything. Faith in the God who had never failed her yet. Anna rose from the bed and thought, *I am going to dare to hope!*

Lord, just as You forgave me of all my offenses, I forgive my loved one for everything that has been done in the past. Even though I do not know what tomorrow may bring, I choose to place my future in Your everlasting mercies. Amen.

THE ASSURANCE OF LOVE

*He heals the brokenhearted and binds
up their wounds [healing their pain
and comforting their sorrow].*
PSALM 147:3 AMP

The little tyke couldn't get enough of his new red bicycle. He rode it as often as his dad would let him. But one day, the boy swerved to miss a cat and landed in a ditch. His father, who was close by, quickly saw that the boy had scraped his knee. Tears ran down the boy's cheek as his dad helped him home. He cleaned his cut, placed a bandage over the wound, and then held him close for a while. Tears subsided as the boy rested in that tender care and the assurance of his father's love. Perhaps there was just as much healing in that hugging as there was in that act of first aid.

In a lifetime we receive many kinds of wounds. But many people would agree that the death of a loved one is one of the hardest to deal with. And yet God is good. He is the binder of wounds—the Great Physician of the body and the mind and the soul. This is what Jesus did as He healed those who came to Him while He was on earth. And that is what Jesus still does even now. No matter the injury. No matter how deep. No matter what.

Reach out to the best Healer of all time. No one can mend your heart like the Lord can. He is longing to care for you, to spend time with you. He's right here, right now. Rest in the assurance of His love.

Lord, I am wounded deeply by my loss. Please transform my mourning into hope and that hope into joy. I am going to put my trust in You, Jesus. Amen.

WEARING THIN

———— ◆ ————

Whoever is slow to anger has great understanding,
but one who has a hasty temper exalts folly.
PROVERBS 14:29 NRSV

Franny sat quietly on the porch swing, since
it had always been a place of refuge for her. Not
really wanting to go anywhere or do anything,
she just wanted to "be" for a while and sort out
her thoughts. Some time had passed since her
husband's funeral, but she had no idea how many
days it had been, because they all drifted together
like a never-ending stream.

Her husband had been a loyal and kind Christian man, yes. But he had a weakness. He couldn't
say no to junk food. Against his own common
sense, he had consumed too much cake, too much
ice cream, and way too many sodas. He hadn't
eaten enough veggies or fruits like he should have,
and he'd never bothered to exercise. Franny had
worried about him and had warned him that his
bad habits would eventually make him sick. Well,
this time, Franny hated that she had been right.

And Franny couldn't help but wonder, *Had*

the man not cared enough for me to change his ways?
His transgressions had felt like a betrayal, but the
seed of anger she felt growing in her spirit also
felt like a betrayal, only this time to God. There
on the swing, Franny cried out, "Lord, just as
my husband committed the sin of gluttony,
I'm succumbing to the sin of bitterness. Please
help me! Even in my grief, I don't want to dis-
please You."

---

*Jesus, my building resentment is wearing
me thin. I don't know where to turn, so I
am going to bring my anger to the foot of the
cross. Please help me leave it there. Amen.*

IT WOULD TAKE A MIRACLE

Whoever restrains his words has knowledge, and he
who has a cool spirit is a man of understanding.
PROVERBS 17:27 ESV

*B*radly knew Christmas was coming, and yet the last thing on his mind was celebrating. There was no room left for rejoicing. Life had dealt him a hard blow—the death of his wife.

The hardships in her life had taken their toll on her. She'd endured the failure of several careers, and they'd been unable to have a family. Both disappointments together had caused a decline in her health. On and off, Bradly had noticed that his wife had been looking rather tired and gaunt, but he had no idea that she was dying. Why hadn't he done something sooner? Why hadn't he paid more attention? Why hadn't his wife's doctor ordered some tests before it was too late? Why had the hospital released her before she was cured? The anger that raged inside him day and night was almost too much to handle. So how was he to rejoice around this sacred holiday? The last thing he felt in his soul was goodwill toward men.

To add to the ordeal, his wife's parents had invited him to spend Christmas Eve at their house. Bradly thought it might be better to be alone. But then again, maybe Christ could help him curb his anger and calm his spirit. It would take a miracle, but then Christ's birth, ministry, and resurrection had all been miraculous, and years before, he had personally known the transforming power of Christ. Yes, Bradly believed that Christ had the power to change him once again.

Lord, help me mourn in a healthy way and help me restrain my words. Even in my sorrow, I want to be a person of knowledge, understanding, and wisdom. Amen.

THE POWER OF GRACE

---

*There is therefore now no condemnation
for those who are in Christ Jesus.*
ROMANS 8:1 ESV

*B*arry's mother, Olivia, had been a great mom in every way. She had been there for him when he was growing up. When he'd broken his arm, trying to conquer the world. When he was diagnosed with depression, when he'd married, and when he'd made it big as a musician. She'd been with him throughout all life's ups and downs, because she was his mom.

And when his mother had asked for one promise—that he never put her into a nursing home—well, he had broken that pledge. As he had feared, Olivia declined very quickly, and six months later she was dead. He could have made a dozen excuses why he had broken his promise, but they all looked tainted with self-interest. He had made a vow to the woman who'd borne him and cared for him and loved him, and he had failed her.

The regret in his spirit was as heavy as stone.

Would he ever recover from the guilt? Would God ever forgive him? Even if God did forgive him, would he ever be able to forgive himself?

Finally, one day he heard a sermon that changed his life. If you are in Christ, there is no condemnation. How could it be? To be free from the past? Truly, *all* of it? If he believed the Bible, then he had to embrace his complete freedom in Christ. Was grace that powerful? The word that returned to him loud and clear was an astounding—*yes!*

———————————————————————

Lord, sometimes I carry a weight of guilt concerning the death of my beloved. Could You remind me of the power of Your grace? Amen.

THE GREATEST HOPE

"He will wipe away every tear from their eyes, and death shall be no more, neither shall there be mourning, nor crying, nor pain anymore, for the former things have passed away."
REVELATION 21:4 ESV

The little girl fell down and scraped her knee. Her mom rushed to her and whispered loving words as she tenderly wiped away the girl's tears. That "wiping away of the tears" gets us every time, right? Just as Revelation 21:4 does.

People go through life trying their best to ignore the impermanence of life on earth. They want to keep the harsh thoughts of mortality at bay. We'd rather think about words like *unsinkable, indomitable, unbeatable,* and *indestructible.* Perhaps we love superheroes because they seem invincible, and we secretly long to live that kind of fantasy where no matter what happens, people simply cannot die.

As Christians, we don't need to long for that fantasy way of life. We don't need to stay so busy and distracted that we won't have time to think about death. We have the living Christ. He rose from the grave, and He conquered death. Once and for all. Christ gets the last say in the matter. And He has promised in His living Word that someday there will be no more dying. No more tears full of sorrow. No more of the pain and suffering that humanity has known since the fall. These will be former things that will pass away.

If we let it, this truth will provide us with courage in times of sorrow. Yes, there is death now, but only for a time. A new era will come. Hope is here. Heaven awaits.

Lord, I thank You that death will one day be banished forever. I believe in Your promises! Amen.

EMBRACING COMPASSION

*Be kind and compassionate to
one another, forgiving each other,
just as in Christ God forgave you.*
EPHESIANS 4:32 NIV

There was no way to put a lighter touch on what Lily had experienced. The miscarriage had been a frightening thing. The sensation of loss and emptiness was even worse. Boxing away her maternity clothes exhausted her, and laying her hand across her empty womb was almost unbearable.

Her husband grieved with her, but still Lily felt isolated in her fluctuating reactions to the loss. Her husband talked of trying for another baby—thought it might cheer her up, he'd said— but Lily's heart still wanted more time to say goodbye to the child she would never know on this side of eternity. The baby she would never cuddle or feed or watch grow up. Then there was the guilt, which was worse than the misunderstandings with her husband. Lily secretly blamed herself for the death of their baby girl, whom she'd named Cloe. Lily kept wondering and worrying, *Did I not eat all the right foods? Did those exercises, which I thought were safe, actually bring on the miscarriage? Did I not pray hard enough or sincerely enough for my baby?* Lily had always strived to be compassionate with all those around her, but this time she thought maybe God was nudging her to show some of that compassion to herself.

Father God, in the midst of my mourning, I am struggling with guilt. Please help me overcome all that I am dealing with. I always try to be compassionate with people around me, but right now I think I need to be compassionate with myself. Could You help me with that right now? In Jesus' powerful name I pray. Amen.

IN THOSE TEARS
CAME HEALING

———— ◆ ————

Now when Mary came to where Jesus was and
saw him, she fell at his feet, saying to him, "Lord,
if you had been here, my brother would not have
died." When Jesus saw her weeping, and the Jews
who had come with her also weeping, he was deeply
moved in his spirit and greatly troubled. And
he said, "Where have you laid him?" They said to
him, "Lord, come and see." Jesus wept. So the
Jews said, "See how he loved him!"

JOHN 11:32–36 ESV

The birthday of their daughter, little May, was
fast approaching, and the grief Craig and his wife
felt over her death was now mixed with anger. The
weight of May's death at the tender age of seven
lay heavily on their hearts. Craig had come from
a family of stoic men, and he felt the best way to
be strong for his wife was to not shed any tears
and to just be there for her. But his wife assumed
that his lack of visible emotion meant that he had
not loved May as much as she had. What Craig

thought was strength and attention she saw as coldness and indifference.

Finally, one evening, Craig and his wife sat down with a pot of coffee and had it out. They talked and argued. They held each other and then talked some more. But most importantly, they wept together. In those tears came the first glimmers of healing. And they made a promise to keep talking, to keep trying to understand, and to keep remembering that it was okay to weep. That even their Savior had wept when faced with the death of someone beloved.

Lord, I am mourning the loss of my loved one.
Help me not to be afraid to weep. Amen.

TENDERNESS AND MERCY

———◆———

For examples of patience in suffering, look at the
Lord's prophets. We know how happy they are now
because they stayed true to him then, even though
they suffered greatly for it. Job is an example of a man
who continued to trust the Lord in sorrow; from his
experiences we can see how the Lord's plan finally
ended in good, for he is full of tenderness and mercy.
JAMES 5:10–11 TLB

*J*ust when Lindsey least expected it, her husband died of a disease she barely knew how to pronounce. Still so young—only thirty-eight!—and yet he was gone, leaving her with two children to raise alone. She'd been a stay-at-home mom, so Lindsey wasn't sure how they would manage, except to try to get a job soon and arrange for some childcare. She had no idea how she would cope on an emotional level, let alone a practical level.

Then Lindsey remembered the many heart cries from the psalms, and feeling desperate and wanting to be real before God, she cried out, "I don't see any purpose here, Lord, or any good coming from my husband's death. I don't see anything but suffering. But in spite of all the grief and uncertainty that I face, I want to show my children I can trust in You, not only in good times, but in times of suffering too. As I wait on You, Lord Jesus, please show me Your tenderness and mercy." One single tear rolled down her cheek. Her heartbeat quieted a little as her soul whispered the truth—God is still there.

Dear Lord, I am in great need of Your tenderness and compassion right now. Please have mercy on me. Amen.

WILL I FORGET?

——— ◆ ———

*Even though I am afflicted and needy, still the Lord
takes thought and is mindful of me. You are my
help and my rescuer. O my God, do not delay.*
Psalm 40:17 amp

*E*rnest watched the yellow bobber gently sway-
ing on the surface of the pond. He doubted
there would be any fish biting today. But then
he didn't really care. A friend had said he needed
to get out into the fresh air and sunlight, and
so he tried to fulfill a promise. Nothing more.
It had been almost four months since his wife's
funeral. The grief wasn't so much lighter as it was
different. Ernest wasn't even sure how to describe
the changes. Sometimes he'd sleep too deeply,
and other times he'd stay awake half the night.
Sometimes he'd even rush to the fireplace mantel
to see his wife's photo because he was afraid that
her face was beginning to fade in his mind. Could
that happen? Would he forget facets of her as
time went on? Like her winsome smile and the
lilt in her voice when she was particularly happy
about life? Or the funny walk she did sometimes

just to make him laugh? Or the compassion she always showed to strangers?

Angry with himself, Ernest reeled in his line. What could he do? To forget his wife felt like a betrayal somehow, and yet to remember her was painful. Ernest hadn't called out to God that often, but he was beginning to think this would be a good time to take his faith more seriously, just as his wife had. Wasn't there a scripture about God being his help and rescuer?

Lord, in my mourning, I have become needy.
Thank You that You are mindful of me.
I need Your divine rescue! Amen.

YOU ARE MY EVERYTHING

"For your Maker is your husband—the LORD Almighty is his name—the Holy One of Israel is your Redeemer; he is called the God of all the earth."

ISAIAH 54:5 NIV

To be heard is a good thing, but to be understood is sublime." That was one of June's favorite quotes, and she always said that of her husband, Aaron, who seemed to be the only person alive who truly understood her. He knew her moods, what upset or delighted her, how terrified she was of snakes and crawly things. All her quirks and foibles and noble strivings. Even more importantly, June considered her husband to be her teammate in life and her best friend in all things. But one cold January day, a rare cancer stole all of that sublime from her. To June, love and death felt like terrible tricks played on her from living in an utterly broken world. She had risked her heart to find love—more than she could ever have imagined—only to have it snatched away.

On one particularly difficult night, June said to God, "I have never felt so frightened and alone as I do now. God, this is a big request, but You are a big God. I need You to be my husband, my helper, my best friend. You have always been my Savior, but now I need You to be my everything. I know You can hear me fully and understand me perfectly because You are my Maker. I cherish Your presence in my life."

Lord Almighty, my Maker, thank You for this promise in Your Holy Word to watch over me like a husband. Thank You for this divine hope in the midst of mourning. In Jesus' name I pray. Amen.

CHRIST'S FORGIVENESS
IS REAL

————————•————————

For God did not send his Son into
the world to condemn the world,
but to save the world through him.
JOHN 3:17 NIV

*W*yatt and Rose had always had a rocky marriage, but despite the many bumps, they loved each other dearly. But on one of those mornings when they refused to see eye to eye, they parted in an angry mood. While Wyatt flew off on a short business trip, Rose drove to work. The devastation Wyatt felt over Rose's death from a drunk driver was compounded by the fact that he hadn't been able to say goodbye. More than that, Wyatt hadn't been able to say he was sorry for their unnecessary argument.

What would he do with all that anger aimed at himself as well as all the weight of guilt? He'd surely disappointed God with his behavior. Wyatt's mind had become like a scene in a movie that wouldn't stop playing. He kept seeing the pain-filled look in Rose's eyes as they parted. He kept hearing their final words together that were born from annoyance and not love. A mere handful of words could have made it right. But pride had gotten the better of him. How could he cope? How could he live with that kind of miserable regret?

A Christian counselor reminded Wyatt that Christ hadn't come to condemn him but to save him. That Christ's forgiveness was real. Another scripture Wyatt clung to was Acts 3:19 (TLB): "Now change your mind and attitude to God and turn to him so he can cleanse away your sins and send you wonderful times of refreshment from the presence of the Lord."

Lord, I need Your forgiveness, Your presence in my life, and those good days of refreshment. Amen.

HIS MERCIES
ENDURE FOREVER

———— ◆ ————

Give thanks to the LORD, for He is good;
for His lovingkindness (graciousness,
mercy, compassion) endures forever.
PSALM 136:1 AMP

Through the years, the Martin family had
passed through many kinds of troubles and sufferings, but when their oldest son took his own
life, the family broke into pieces. Their dear son—
who was a Christ follower—could not seem to
deal with the bouts of depression he suffered.
After the Martin family's shock and anger faded,
they headed through a long chapter of guilt.
When they gathered together, they continued to
ask one another countless questions: What could
I have done differently? Could I have contri-
buted to his depression? Had I said the wrong
words? Had I been too judgmental or demanding?
Did I not encourage him enough to get help?
Did I not pray for him enough? Did I not listen
or laugh or understand enough? . . . The guilt of a

thousand queries became a daily affliction.

As the Martin family pondered their pain and cried out in their distress, they finally chose to leave all their questions and fears in the hands of the Lord. From past experiences, they knew Him to be full of compassion and graciousness, forgiving not just a few sins but all transgressions. They would have to trust in Christ's mercy or nothing at all. They chose to believe.

The family also adopted Philippians 4:7 (AMP) as their family verse: "And the peace of God [that peace which reassures the heart, that peace] which transcends all understanding, [that peace which] stands guard over your hearts and your minds in Christ Jesus [is yours]."

Lord, there are so many painful things in this life I do not understand. But I am going to trust You in Your promise to provide a peace that transcends all understanding. Amen.

THE LORD IS NEAR

*I am always thinking of the Lord; and because
he is so near, I never need to stumble or fall.*
PSALM 16:8 TLB

Camille sat down with her neighbor over some fresh-brewed coffee. It was Camille's first social outing since her husband died. Camille listened mostly. She nibbled cake, sipped her beverage, and smiled at her neighbor's ongoing chatter. Then out of the blue, her neighbor said, "Wow, you sure seem to be recovering fast. Hope I can snap back that quickly when my husband dies."

Camille wasn't sure what to do with that statement, since it came off sort of callous in a number of ways. At first, she wanted to blow off the comment with a wave, but then a flash of anger flared up in her. After a calming pause, Camille responded, "I loved my husband very much. I *am* grieving, but I think that people go through the process in different ways. And too, people have different temperaments. When I do feel a wave of grief, I force my mind to think about the Lord. Eventually the gloomy thoughts start to lift."

Later at home, Camille thought it was interesting that during her time of mourning, the anger she sometimes felt hadn't been against God or the doctors or even herself. But she had been irritated by the insensitivity of people who, during a crisis, seemed to feel obligated to speak without thought or love.

Camille wanted to offer them all a bit of advice—"If you desire to create a healing environment for the mourner, sometimes silence goes a long way."

---

*Lord, help me forgive all those who are doing
and saying things that offend me as I grieve.
Help me see that most people have good intentions,
and help me speak the truth in love. Amen.*

THE HOPE WE HAVE

*And now, dear brothers, I want you to know what
happens to a Christian when he dies so that when it
happens, you will not be full of sorrow, as those are
who have no hope. For since we believe that Jesus
died and then came back to life again, we can also
believe that when Jesus returns, God will bring
back with him all the Christians who have died.*

1 Thessalonians 4:13–14 TLB

As Christians we possess something that the
world cannot ever reproduce or destroy—and that
is hope in Christ. We wake up, walk through our
day, and go to bed at night with hope. It changes
the way we view our everyday choices and what
we do with our time, our money, and the talents
and gifts that He's given us. It influences the way
we raise our kids. The way we talk and disagree
and vote and play and worship. That hope in
Christ not only changes how we live, but it also
alters the way we die. The way we mourn. The
way we look up toward the heavens and smile,
knowing that our seed of hope as a Christ follower
will one day burst into life eternal.

And while we wait for the glories of God's kingdom, we can live with this promise from Romans 8:28 (VOICE): "We are confident that God is able to orchestrate everything to work toward something good and beautiful when we love Him and accept His invitation to live according to His plan."

Yes, God is ever watching out for us—in our living and in our dying.

Almighty God, words will never be enough to express my gratitude that You sent Your Son that we might have life forever with You. I embrace the grace and claim that glorious hope! In Jesus' name I pray. Amen.

LOVINGLY ACTIVE

Save me, O God! For the waters have come up to my neck. I sink in deep mire, where there is no foothold; I have come into deep waters, and the flood sweeps over me. I am weary with my crying out; my throat is parched. My eyes grow dim with waiting for my God.

PSALM 69:1–3 ESV

"My sister died, Lord. Where were You, and where are You now?" was the prayer that came from a woman named Nelly. Her beloved younger sister had passed away suddenly, and she was left heart-stricken with grief. Nelly's beseeching prayers continued. "Lord, my sister had her life planned out with dreams that You had designed and set into motion! Is this our reward for faithfulness? If even the noblest life can get snuffed out decades too early, then what is the point?"

Nelly soon wondered about her own purpose and began doubting the meaning of life. Her existence suddenly seemed haphazard and fearsomely out of control. It felt as if the Designer of earth and humans had packed up and gone somewhere else, leaving everyone to find their own way.

The Bible shows us many lamenting cries to God such as the one in Psalm 69. But we also read many verses that praise the Lord for His mighty rescues. Will everyone have every prayer answered the way he or she would like? No; even Jesus wasn't rescued from His sufferings. But because of Christ's willing sacrifice on the cross for the redemption of sins, we as believers can be assured that God is most definitely not absent from our lives or merely passively interested in our affairs. Yes, throughout the ages and even in this very hour, God is powerfully present and lovingly active!

Thank You, Lord, that even in my sorrow,
You are intimately involved in my life! Amen.

ALL THE LIGHT AND LOVE

———●———

Later, in one of his talks, Jesus said to the people,
"I am the Light of the world. So if you follow me,
you won't be stumbling through the darkness,
for living light will flood your path."
JOHN 8:12 TLB

*B*everly's mom had always been a bighearted woman. She gave of her life freely, and her love for people was pleasantly received everywhere she went. She also had the unique gift of knowing how to create a beautiful moment. Her mom could cook up a French meal nearly in her sleep. She could dress a table like a queen, and she could paint almost like a master. Her mom was a woman with many talents, and she lavishly used them for God's glory. She was a woman you just loved being around.

And that was some of what Beverly wrote in her eulogy about her mother. But when she got home after the funeral and realized once again that all that beauty and love was gone from her life—all that light and laughter had been snuffed out—anger crept into her heart.

When Beverly reached the pinnacle of her emotions, she remembered God. That the Lord had been the One to create such a remarkable woman, and that He was the One who had granted Beverly the right to call her Mom and friend. Beverly said, "God, thank You for those many years with my mom. Even in my sorrow, I will continue to trust in You. In Your promises, Your love, and Your living light."

Dear God, in my darkest hours of mourning, remind me of Your love and continue to keep me in Your divine presence. May I rise up each day with hope in my soul. In Jesus' name I pray. Amen.

GOD DOESN'T FAIL

———— ◆ ————

"Don't be afraid, for the Lord will go before you and will be with you; he will not fail nor forsake you."
DEUTERONOMY 31:8 TLB

The ruby ring that had been in Sally's family for generations really wasn't worth a great deal of money, but nevertheless, the heirloom meant a great deal to her. The piece of jewelry was a treasure of the heart, since it had belonged to her dear grandmother who'd gone on to heaven. According to her parents, they had all wanted Sally to have the ring to show how much they loved her and how proud they were of her. But when both her parents had passed on, Sally was confused as to why the ring had suddenly been sold before they'd died. Had her parents fallen on hard times and needed the money? Had they changed their minds about giving it to her? Had they not been so proud of her after all? Or maybe they'd simply forgotten their promise. Yes, she had gotten some inheritance, but that ring represented something far more important to her. It would have expressed volumes of their love and their pride and their joy in her future.

As much as she had loved her parents, Sally was brokenhearted and a little angry over the incident. She would never know why her parents had neglected their promise. In the midst of her grieving, she would forgive them, of course. But Sally was glad that in her time of sorrow her God would never fail her, and that He would always keep His promises.

Father God, I realize that humans fail us,
even those we love, but I thank You that
Your love is never careless or disappointing.
In Jesus' name I pray. Amen.

DON'T BE AFRAID

Shortly before dawn Jesus went out to them, walking on the lake. When the disciples saw him walking on the lake, they were terrified. "It's a ghost," they said, and cried out in fear. But Jesus immediately said to them: "Take courage! It is I. Don't be afraid." "Lord, if it's you," Peter replied, "tell me to come to you on the water." "Come," he said. Then Peter got down out of the boat, walked on the water and came toward Jesus. But when he saw the wind, he was afraid and, beginning to sink, cried out, "Lord, save me!" Immediately Jesus reached out his hand and caught him. "You of little faith," he said, "why did you doubt?"

MATTHEW 14:25–31 NIV

*B*ecause this world is so profoundly broken, we will undoubtedly come to know sorrow sometimes during our lifetime. Some of it will relate to failures, misunderstandings, cruelties, disloyalties, abandonment, and the death of our loved ones. You might say, "So much pain! How can anyone's spirit survive it all?" We were meant for the joy of Eden, not this sin, despair, and death. We can't handle it really—without the help of Christ.

When Peter saw Jesus walking on the lake, he wanted to meet Jesus there on the water. He surely wanted to show his loyalty and his love. But the moment Peter's eyes drifted off to the thrashing winds and the raging waves, he became frightened and began to sink. But even in the disciple's doubts, Jesus immediately came to his rescue.

If you are afraid in your sorrow, take heart. Jesus is there. Grasp His hand. It is strong enough to take you through the thrashing winds of doubt and the raging waves of fear.

Lord, be with me in this terrible grief.
I need Your mighty hand of rescue. Amen.

THIS SACRED PASSAGE!

Listen to me, all of you in far-off lands:
The Lord called me before my birth. From
within the womb he called me by my name.
ISAIAH 49:1 TLB

After conception, your heartbeat could be heard as early as the eighteenth day. As God weaved you in your mother's womb—there in that inner well of life—He knew you by name. Imagine! The world does not always see life as precious, but God does. People are priceless, and life is a treasure, and so are those moments when you say goodbye to your beloved. And so are the waves of mourning. And so are the many years of remembrance. To hold up your loved one with honor, acknowledging him or her as an eternal being made in the image of God, is right and good.

If society ever makes you feel that you must run from grief, don't believe it. To lament over someone's death means you cared. It shows how much you risked your heart and how well you loved. These cherished sentiments cannot be swept away with death, nor should they be. God is pleased when we love, and to choose to delight the Lord in the way we live and love is no small thing.

To weep and express sorrow is also to know the heart of Christ, for He too knew suffering and He too wept. As you take the time to go through this sacred passage called bereavement, know that God cares greatly, even more than you do. And God weeps with you.

Lord, I have loved greatly, and I am grieving deeply. Thank You for staying close to me and for weeping along with me. It is a comfort. I love You. Amen.

GIVE ME A TENDER HEART

———————

*Be kind to one another, tenderhearted, forgiving
one another, as God in Christ forgave you.*
EPHESIANS 4:32 ESV

*C*andice had tried to be the best of daughters because she loved her parents and she loved her God. But after her mom died, she became the sole caretaker of her father, and that sacrificial task had turned out to be harder than Candice ever imagined. Her father had suffered with dementia, and what should have been a sweet time of grow ing closer to him became a season of spiteful deeds and cruel words poured out to her.

After his funeral, Candice fell on her knees by her bed in total exhaustion and cried out to the Lord, "I meant for this time of caregiving for my father to be special, but You know that it did not end well. My father no longer even knew who I was. At times his temper would flare for no reason. At times my father seemed to almost hate me. Lord, give me a tender and forgiving heart. Help me remember that my father didn't mean what he said. That he was riddled with an illness in his mind that he couldn't control. And Lord, I confess that in those times when I was being mistreated, I too gave in to anger and harsh words against him. For that I am truly sorry. Help me remember all the good times I had with my dad growing up, and help those good memories to comfort me in my time of mourning. Please give me a renewed love for my dad and for You."

Dearest Lord, forgive me for the times I have not been all I should have been for my loved one. Thank You for Your mercy and grace. Amen.

TO WALK WITH GOD

———◆———

*"Be still, and know that I am God. I will be exalted
among the nations, I will be exalted in the earth!"*
PSALM 46:10 ESV

*D*arrell had always been a man who knew
how to walk with God and how to grow in his
faith. And then his wife of thirty-eight years died.
Darrell passed through a time of doubt and a
season of anger. Anger at the world, his friends,
and even God. He had always hoped and even
prayed that he would go to heaven first so that he
would never have to know what it would be like
to live on this earth without his beloved. Darrell
had never wanted to know a moment of that
feeling, let alone years. But here he was alone
without her. And all his friends could think to
say was, "Even in the midst of your grief, couldn't
you try to carve out a little joy for yourself?" But
Darrell wondered how he could do that when
nothing was right and nothing ever would be.
His life had fallen apart, and he couldn't imagine
how it could be put back together.

But one day when Darrell's bleakness of spirit

was nearly overtaking him, he took a walk through the meadow behind his house. He looked up and prayed the simplest prayers asking for a moment of peace and for the smallest ray of joy. The sun broke through the clouds and warmed his face. Darrell rested in the meadow and took some time that day to be still before God. Could the Lord be telling him that even in his misery he could be at peace? That he could come to rely on the Lord for everything? Even now?

Lord, no matter what, may we always walk this earthly path together. Amen.

WE ARE TRULY FORGIVEN

*If we [freely] admit that we have sinned and
confess our sins, He is faithful and just [true to
His own nature and promises], and will forgive
our sins and cleanse us continually from all
unrighteousness [our wrongdoing, everything not
in conformity with His will and purpose].*

1 JOHN 1:9 AMP

With the loss of a spouse, some people may
ask, "If I had done something differently, could
my spouse still be alive?" Sometimes a measure of
guilt will tag along with this question and torture
our days and torment our nights.

Even if in some way we had been neglectful
toward our loved one, God forgives. Not just for
the transgressions that may appear easy to forgive,
but for everything. God is in the business of
redemption. Through Christ we can be forgiven
for all our sins, no matter what they are.

Then once you are forgiven, let them go.
Move on. The enemy will try to bring forgiven
sins before you time and time again, not with a
holy objective, but for the purpose of producing

condemnation, confusion, and fear. Have no part in the enemy's plot to derail or destroy you.

May you instead embrace the truth of Christ's grace and may you bask in the glorious freedom of His mercy. May your mourning not be clouded with guilt, but may it instead be filled with plentiful love, fond memories, and the gentle peace that passes all understanding.

Lord, God Almighty, I thank You for being faithful and just in every way and for being true to Your many promises. Thank You that when I repent, You are willing to cleanse me from all unrighteousness. In Jesus' holy name I pray. Amen.

FINDING GOOD JUDGMENT

———— ◆ ————

Teach me good judgment (discernment)
and knowledge, for I have believed and
trusted and relied on Your commandments.
PSALM 119:66 AMP

*W*hen Julianna got the news that her uncle
had died of old age, it wasn't a surprise, but it was
certainly painful nevertheless. But because the
service was so far away, she chose to stay home.
Several of the family members heaped some pretty
heavy guilt on Julianna for not attending her
uncle's memorial service. The grief of losing her
uncle had been an unhappy event in itself,
because she had loved him, but to have the sadness compounded with guilt made it almost
overwhelming. Was Julianna truly required to
be there? Had she hurt her family that deeply, or
were they just lashing out because they too were
dealing with the loss?

It was a forlorn fact, but Julianna did notice
that the older she got, the more funerals there
were to attend. What was the right thing to do?
She couldn't attend them all or travel to them all.

Was it appropriate sometimes to send condolences with flowers and cards or a phone call?

Wanting to have a godly response, Julianna finally gave the dilemma to God. She knew He could handle it. She prayed that the Holy Spirit would give her discernment in the matter. Not just in how to compassionately deal with funerals and the surviving loved ones, but how to handle all of life. She knew that to seek God in all her comings and goings meant to live lovingly and freely.

Holy Spirit, I trust You. Please give me clear discernment concerning how to handle funerals and how to deal with every aspect of my life. I cherish Your guidance. Amen.

REST

———————— ◆ ————————

*"Come to me and I will give you rest—all of you
who work so hard beneath a heavy yoke. Wear my
yoke—for it fits perfectly—and let me teach you;
for I am gentle and humble, and you shall find rest
for your souls; for I give you only light burdens."*
MATTHEW 11:28 TLB

*L*eo had never been a wealthy man, but he had
always said—as the old saying went—that he was
rich when it came to love. His wife had meant
more to him than words could ever say. So, when
she died in the hospital of pneumonia, he nearly
collapsed right there in grief. How could it have
happened? The love of his life? Gone.

Even though planning his wife's funeral now
seemed like a blur months later, Leo remembered
some parts of it with perfect clarity. He remembered being pressured—in subtle ways and some
not-so-subtle ways—to spend more on the funeral
than he felt was suitable for his income. All anyone needed to say was, "We know you want the
best for your wife," and he was tempted to go
into debt to make a truly spectacular service for

his beloved. In the end, he had chosen not to overspend. Leo and his wife had always chosen to be frugal, and that wisdom had always paid off in the long run.

But now that his wife had been gone for a while and he was left only with photographs and his memories, he had begun to feel some guilt over his choices. Should he have spent more on the funeral? When Leo prayed about it, though, Matthew 11:28 always came to mind. Again and again, the Lord said, "Come to me and I will give you rest."

Lord, thank You for giving me
rest in times of sorrow. Amen.

JUST A BIT OF KINDNESS

———————•———————

Love each other with brotherly affection
and take delight in honoring each other.
ROMANS 12:10 TLB

Zoe felt like she was on the edge of despair. Her heart craved kindness, since she believed what had just happened to her child should not have happened. No mother should even have to think about it. For a child to die was unthinkable. And now, during the unthinkable—which was now her reality—people were coming to her nonstop with words. So many words. And none of them really spoke to her. None of the speeches seemed to hold kindness or healing. Just advice. And judgment. And empty promises. And trite comments. And sweeping opinions. And words like, "Honey, I know just how you feel." Her mind wanted to scream, "Don't say that! How could you know? You have never lost a child. A child never should die before the mother or the father." In fact, come to think of it, Zoe wondered if she had indeed screamed it in the midst of her blinding grief. God help her. If people could only offer empty talk, then what she needed was silence! She needed some good thinking time and praying time. And she needed tears. Yes, plenty of tears. And in the meantime, Zoe prayed that the people who came to her would be patient and compassionate and full of godly affection. That they would be the kind of people who delighted in honoring each other.

Father God, I sometimes feel as though I am getting swallowed up by grief. Please be ever near me, and help the people who are trying to bring me comfort. Give them a servant's heart, supernatural wisdom, and a listening ear. In Jesus' holy name I pray. Amen.

INTO THE ARMS OF LOVE

For God has not given us a spirit of fear,
but of power and of love and of a sound mind.
2 TIMOTHY 1:7 NKJV

*N*o one knew about the young man's addiction. Not even Jolene and Ross, his parents. They were shocked to learn that their adult son had been addicted to pain pills. They didn't find out until it was too late—when their only son was dead from an accidental overdose.

Jolene and Ross felt tormented, responsible somehow, and yet they'd had no previous hints that their son had been hooked on those meds. The prescription crisis people talked about was indeed that, a crisis, and yet it was a silent killer too. Jolene and Ross felt they might never survive their loss or the anger against a shameless and greedy industry that could perpetuate such a travesty. Hate rose up in them both, fear weighted their souls, and at times they felt that the injustice and despair of it all could cause them to lose their minds.

But one evening in the height of sorrow, the

couple bowed their heads. They turned to God, wanting to trust the Lord even in the midst of calamity and confusion and rage. They memorized 2 Timothy 1:7 and said it out loud whenever they had need.

They knew that on their own they could not survive the onslaught of pain, but somehow, step by step, they would trust the Lord with their anguish. After all, God also knew what it was like to lose His Son—His only Son. So, Jolene and Ross both gave up their hold on the future and surrendered themselves into the arms of love.

Dearest Lord Jesus, please comfort me in this deepest hurt. I will put my trust in You. Amen.

EVERLASTING LOVE

—————◆—————

The LORD appeared to us in the past, saying:
"I have loved you with an everlasting love;
I have drawn you with unfailing kindness."
JEREMIAH 31:3 NIV

Maryellen never imagined that the words "I survived the car crash" would ever be tinged with such bewilderment and guilt, but deep in her soul she felt the stain of those emotions in her heart. She wondered why she had been the one to survive. She and her best friend had been out to have a bite of dinner at their favorite café, and on the way home there had been the slightest patch of ice on one of the bridges. It was such a mystery. Spring had arrived, and there were no clues of lingering frost and no forecast of icy conditions. And yet there it was, glassy and deadly. Enough to kill her dearest friend in the world.

Maryellen kept asking herself, *Why was I the one to survive? Why me?* She thought of herself as a Christian, but her dear friend had been the most committed follower of Christ she'd ever known. Her friend went on mission trips, fed the homeless at their local shelter, and took great delight in her Lord. Maryellen thought that if anyone should have died that evening it should have been her, not her friend.

When Maryellen's thoughts kept haunting her, she tried to do what her friend would have done—she prayed. She knew she would need some serious help to walk through this frightening ordeal, so she asked the Lord to be especially near to her. She asked that His everlasting love would surround her and warm her soul, and that His unfailing kindness would lighten her load on this journey.

***

Lord, I need to feel Your everlasting love.
Be ever near me in these times of suffering. Amen.

STREAMS IN THE DESERT

He was despised and rejected by men, a Man of sorrows and pain and acquainted with grief; and like One from whom men hide their faces He was despised, and we did not appreciate His worth or esteem Him.
ISAIAH 53:3 AMP

Imagine the driest, most barren wasteland you've ever seen. Winds howl and darkness falls. It feels as though the idea of new life in such a place could never be more than a pretty notion, a long-forgotten dream. That is sometimes how depression feels—desolate and lonely.

Know that you are not alone in your troubled emotions. Jesus knew grief well. He was even called "a Man of sorrows." He walked this earth, and He allowed Himself to know the pain of humanity. Not to witness it from afar, as some cold and curious deity, but to truly share in our lives and our burdens—and then to save us from the frightening prospect of living life in a perpetual wilderness. When Christ came, He brought refreshing, cooling rains to this thirsty, desertscape of our souls. And then came new life and real growth and blossoming beauty.

Isaiah 43:19 (TLB) reminds us, "For I'm going to do a brand-new thing. See, I have already begun! Don't you see it? I will make a road through the wilderness of the world for my people to go home, and create rivers for them in the desert!"

Yes, even in our times of sorrow and sadness—yes, even then—thank God that nothing can take away this promise of a road through the wilderness and His streams in the desert!

Dear Lord, my soul is in a sad and desolate place. Please show me the road I should take, and please bring me to those refreshing streams in the desert. Amen.

AS SURE AS THE DAWN

———◆———

*"Let us acknowledge the LORD; let us press on
to acknowledge him. As surely as the sun rises,
he will appear; he will come to us like the winter
rains, like the spring rains that water the earth."*
HOSEA 6:3 NIV

*M*arla was distraught when her husband of twenty-three years died unexpectedly. She didn't know what to do with her grief, so she chose to stay home and try to work through her loss as best she could. But then after depression and loneliness settled in, Marla decided it would be best to get out of the house for a little while. Unfortunately, none of her friends seemed interested in joining her. They offered excuses such as, "I can't grab lunch tomorrow, but check back with me in a couple of weeks." Or, "Yes, let's set something up." But then her friends would never call back. Marla thought, *Do they think death is catching?* Or perhaps they feared she would spend too much time talking about her husband's passing. Or maybe her friends thought she'd beg them for money! Whatever was wrong, her friends made her feel discarded. Marla didn't really know what to do next.

Except maybe she could spend time with her God. Yes, that she could do. So, Marla prayed, "I'm suffering from depression, Lord, and I need You to bless me with some good and loyal earthly friends. Thank You for Your never-ending care and attention. Your friendship is true and beautiful. Help me keep pressing on to know You better, for Your Word reminds me that Your appearing is as sure as the dawn, and You are as refreshing as the showers of springtime."

*Lord, I thank You for being
a friend always. Amen.*

I WILL BE WITH YOU!

———————•———————

*"I have told you these things, so that in me you may
have peace. In this world you will have trouble.
But take heart! I have overcome the world."*
JOHN 16:33 NIV

*H*ave you ever had a crisis of faith? It can be
a tidal wave of doubt that suddenly overwhelms
you or it can be a slow *drip, drip, drip* of nagging
uncertainties that build up over time. The loss of
someone you love can bring you to that point
of crisis. But the Lord still cares for you deeply,
and He reminds you that, yes, while you will
have trouble in this life, you can know peace in
Him because He has overcome the world. This
truth can hold you steady during times when the
world and its trials threaten to shake your faith to
its core. Or it can help you to rebuild your faith
from the rubble that used to be your strong wall
of faith in Christ.

Remember even when your soul feels frail
and faltering, Isaiah 43:2 (ESV) encourages you
by saying, "When you pass through the waters, I
will be with you; and through the rivers, they shall

not overwhelm you; when you walk through fire you shall not be burned, and the flame shall not consume you."

Take heart. If you pass through the deep waters of sorrow or you walk through the fiery tribulations of doubt that may come in their wake, cling to the Almighty. His love is real, and His promises are full of power and might.

Lord, I am so weary, and my trust in You is faltering. Please restore my faith, refresh my spirit, and bring me to a place of peace. Amen.

TEARS IN A BOTTLE

*You have kept count of my tossings; put my tears in
your bottle. Are they not in your book?*
PSALM 56:8 ESV

*Y*ou toss and turn, dampening your pillow
with tears again. How long? Will it never stop?
The shock of losing your beloved was hard, but
that ongoing lonely ache deep in your being, well,
no one told you how bad that was going to be.
You long to be with people, and yet all the people
in the world cannot replace your dear one. All the
joys and pleasures cooked up by mankind cannot
seem to keep you distracted from your sorrow.
You simply want the clock to be turned back and
for all that was taken from you to be returned.

You cry out to God. Does He understand?
Does He care? A friend mails you a card, and in it
there is that unique verse—Psalm 56:8—and you
think, *So, you mean God knows of all my sleepless
nights and the weeping of my soul? He keeps my tears
in a bottle? He knows the whys of every one?*

Perhaps this verse is like a love letter from
God—a note to remind you that while we suffer

a little while on this broken earth, one day this bottle of tears will be broken and sorrow and weeping will be no more.

May this verse be like a fragrant perfume to your soul. And in those troubled hours of the night, may you always breathe in the sweet encouragement of it.

I am uplifted by Your love, Lord, that You care for every detail of my life. Please be ever near me in my sadness and loneliness that comes from my great loss. Amen.

A HOPE AND A FUTURE

For surely I know the plans I have for you,
says the LORD, plans for your welfare and
not for harm, to give you a future with hope.
JEREMIAH 29:11 NRSV

*A*fter Marcus recovered from the shock waves of losing his wife, a lingering sadness settled into his spirit. The depression was made worse by the fear that he would forget his sweetheart altogether. His wife's lovely face was already fading a little in his mind's eye, and the fond memories seemed a little more distant. Marcus thought, *My wife does not deserve to be forgotten, so I will keep all of it fresh in my mind.* Yet constantly facing the remembrances of "what once was" seemed almost unbearable. His feelings told him that there was no solution, no future, no hope, and yet Marcus knew that feelings could be misleading. He clung to the scripture "For surely I know the plans I have for you, says the LORD, plans for your welfare and not for harm, to give you a future with hope."

We don't know all the details of what tomorrow will bring, but we can safely put our future in the Lord's hands. Even in our loss and depression and lonesomeness, we must come to a point of choice—whom do we trust? We can read the answer to the question of our souls in Psalm 39:7 (AMP), "And now, Lord, for what do I expectantly wait? My hope [my confident expectation] is in You."

God still has a plan for you, a holy calling. Draw peace from this truth whenever you have need.

Lord, show me Your plan and Your purpose for me. I need Your strong hand to lift me up and Your holy guidance to show me the way. Amen.

THE COMFORTER

"If you love me, obey me; and I will ask the Father and he will give you another Comforter, and he will never leave you."
JOHN 14:16 TLB

*F*or Jill, the day had been yet another long and tiresome one. She'd driven home in heavy traffic and then curled up on the living room couch. Instead of making dinner, she wanted to spend a little time thinking about the wonderful man she'd been happily married to for decades. Her husband had been gone for some months, and oh, how she missed him—his wisdom and banter and laughter. In fact, the house had gone so quiet for so long that it gave her heart an ache. She understood that the kids had their own full lives now, so she didn't expect daily calls. The neighbors no longer dropped by with casseroles and conversation. And her coworkers kept hinting at the idea of moving on from her mourning.

Jill discovered that grief wasn't easy to let go of, but she wondered if in years to come all the tragic pieces might get woven into the fabric of her life like other experiences. Each life piece would be very different, of course—some light, some colorful, and some very dark—but altogether, even with the inky black patches, God could make something beautiful out of it. Jill reached for her favorite quilt and pulled it up over her shoulders. Suddenly, she remembered that before Jesus left this earth, He promised to send the Comforter.

Jill prayed to the Holy Spirit, that He would be like a quilt around her soul, warming her, comforting her, and bringing her peace. Jill fell asleep thinking of the light and love of the One who would never leave her.

Thank You, Lord, for the comfort of Your Holy Spirit. Amen.

IN THE HANDS OF A MERCIFUL GOD

Now we do not want you to be uninformed,
believers, about those who are asleep [in death],
so that you will not grieve [for them] as the others
do who have no hope [beyond this present life].
1 Thessalonians 4:13 AMP

The dawn arrived! It appeared first as a blue backdrop, silhouetting a grove of evergreens. Then the morning twilight ever so slowly paled, giving the celestial bodies a mystical twinkle. But then as if the Creator said this wasn't enough majesty for us to delight in, He floated in some skippy seraphim-like clouds and set them on fire as the sun rose in a blaze of glory. Yes, He is the Creator of breathless wonder. Beautiful mystery and mighty power are His. Perfect grace and unfathomable mercy—oh, that is our God. And that is the same God who created you and your loved one. If we can trust Him with the dawn, then we can trust Him with our beloved. As it says in 1 Thessalonians, we do not need to grieve as others who have no hope beyond this present life. As believers, we have the promise of heaven.

Some people may suffer with the added grief of not knowing about the spiritual status of their beloved, but people who are dying often come to Christ at the last moment—just as the man did who hung on the cross next to Christ. We do not always know what our loved ones came to believe at the last moments of their lives. So, it is best to leave everything—even what is unknown to us— in the hands of a merciful God.

Oh Lord, I know You are in control of everything. I am going to trust You with my beloved and with my life as well! Amen.

DON'T BE AFRAID

------◆------

*When Simon Peter saw this, he fell at Jesus' knees
and said, "Go away from me, Lord; I am a sinful
man!" For he and all his companions were astonished
at the catch of fish they had taken, and so were James
and John, the sons of Zebedee, Simon's partners.
Then Jesus said to Simon, "Don't be afraid;
from now on you will fish for people."*
LUKE 5:8–10 NIV

*O*ne of the lies of the enemy is to make us
believe that we have strayed too far spiritually to
ever go back into the presence of the Lord. That
our thoughts and actions and words have been
too dark to be forgiven. That in our grief we
have become such a sad heap of humanity that
expecting to be welcomed back with open arms is
unthinkable.

Never believe that lie. You can go back. Even
when you doubted God? Yes. Even when you
shook your fist at Him after your beloved died?
Yes. Even when you got so depressed you wanted
to take your own life? Yes to all the above.

In the book of Luke, we discover that when

Peter first met Jesus, he didn't even want the Lord to look upon him. Peter believed he was too great of a sinner to stand in the Lord's presence. And yet Peter was destined to become a great apostle for Christ.

God loves you and wants to take you back right now. In fact, the Lord is longing to take you back, to forgive you, to love you, to commune with you. Run into His mighty and tender arms. Don't be afraid. Trust in Him for everything— even the darkest hours of your life.

Lord, I come into Your presence just as I am, broken by this world. Please help me. Amen.

THE AUTHOR OF LOVE

---

*Whoever does not love does not
know God, because God is love.*
1 John 4:8 niv

*A*fter the death of your spouse, perhaps you're
thinking, *We created this thing of beauty between us.
Together we made a beautiful marriage full of love
and light. Birthed some great kids. Made a happy
home. Yes, a good life. So, now the light seems to be
gone—all that beauty and love and life snatched up
by death.*

But God created you and your spouse. God is
the Author of love, and He is the One who created
all that love and beauty and light. He is the One
who gave you all those good gifts, including your
relationship and marriage and kids. And the God
who blessed you with everything is still there. He
has never changed, nor will He. Reach out to the
Lord. He knows. He cares. Abide in the everlasting
arms of love.

First John 4:16 (tlb) tells us so beautifully,
"We know how much God loves us because we
have felt his love and because we believe him when

he tells us that he loves us dearly. God is love, and anyone who lives in love is living with God and God is living in him."

Almighty God, I have loved so deeply, and now I feel lost and alone. But I choose to put my faith in You, since I know You are the Author of love and the Designer of this holy tradition of marriage. Help me know that You still love me and that You will be ever near me in my sadness and loneliness. And remind me that one day, in Your perfect timing, You will love me right into heaven. In Jesus' name I pray. Amen.

I WILL HELP YOU!

———————————

Fear not, for I am with you. Do not be dismayed.
I am your God. I will strengthen you; I will help you;
I will uphold you with my victorious right hand.

ISAIAH 41:10 TLB

The day has come—a day you've dreaded for months since your husband's funeral. The time has come for you to let go of some of his possessions, and yet you hesitate. There in the closets and attic and basement is an epic amount of living—collecting and storing and treasuring and enjoying. But now you will need to sift through all of it and decide what to give away, what to throw away, and what to keep as cherished heirlooms and objects of remembrance. That sorting process seems like an impossible task, really, because it feels disrespectful in some way—as if all that epic living will now be diminished or even forgotten. But since you need to move into a smaller house now, you feel there is no choice but to scale down on your belongings.

When you step into his closet, though, and you catch a whiff of your husband's cologne, suddenly you're tempted to close the door and keep everything as it was. But the reality is that nothing can be as it was. Everything has already changed. So, trembling and lonely and scared, you sit down on the floor and pray. And you pray some more. Until you feel the warmth of tears, the nearness of God, and the strength to take one more step.

Lord, I feel I am ready to begin the process of accepting my loss, but I am afraid of all the tasks that I have before me. Please help me with every single step. I need You in every moment, every breath. Amen.

CHOOSE FRIENDS WISELY

———•———

*The man of too many friends [chosen
indiscriminately] will be broken in pieces and
come to ruin, but there is a [true, loving] friend
who [is reliable and] sticks closer than a brother.*
PROVERBS 18:24 AMP

S ometimes we try to be like islands in the sea.
We might try solitude even when our hearts tell us
it's impossible. God made us for fellowship with
Him and with others.

Somewhere in our sorrow we will need to
reach out to friends. Otherwise the loneliness and
depression that can come from grief may become
too much for us. Reach out. But be wise in that
choice of friends.

Have you gone on social media and wanted
to find fellowship there? Has it been fulfilling, or
does it make you feel more isolated and depressed?
If so, let it go. Move on from the cyber world.
There is nothing quite like real hugs and real
conversation with real friends to lift one's spirit
and make the heart feel a little less lonesome.

Have your current friends been loyal and

compassionate while you've been grieving your loss? Or do you have too many friends that you may have chosen too hastily? Are some of your relationships hurting you more than they are helping and healing? If so, ask God to provide you with good and godly friends who can help you in your time of need. Even Jesus had friends while He was on this earth. Fellowship can not only be beautiful; it is vital.

Father God, I am in need of a few good earthly friends. Help me find them or them to find me. I am going to trust You to supply all my needs. In Jesus' name I pray. Amen.

WHO AM I?

———— ❖ ————

But to as many as did receive and welcome Him,
He gave the right [the authority, the privilege] to
become children of God, that is, to those who believe
in (adhere to, trust in, and rely on) His name.
John 1:12 AMP

*B*ella had been a work-at-home wife for decades, and she had not only taken her various tasks seriously; she had also loved them. She grew fresh garden produce and volunteered for prolife organizations and charities for the homeless, and she loved opening her home up to all those who needed her. Bella admired the biblical character Tabitha and had wanted to incorporate some of those noble qualities into her daily life.

But now that her husband had gone on to heaven and she was alone, the work no longer had the spark that it once had. In fact, some mornings it was hard to get out of bed. She didn't feel up to making big meals or cleaning the house or weeding the garden or doing the volunteer work. Not only did Bella wonder how to move forward, but it felt as though she'd lost some of her identity.

Bella thought, *Who am I anyway? And who will I be from now on?*

Maybe she needed to get back to the basics. Bella remembered the scripture in John that reminded her of who she was in Christ. She was a child of God. That had not changed. She still had that privilege and honor. And it was a great one. All was not lost. True, she was no longer an earthly wife, but she was still a child of the living Lord. Bella thought, *God can work with that.*

===

Lord, help me remember that as a Christian, I am still Your child! Amen.

A TENDERNESS OF THE SOUL

You should defend those who cannot help themselves. Yes, speak up for the poor and helpless, and see that they get justice.

PROVERBS 31:8–9 TLB

*E*ric walked by a homeless man on the street, and for the first time he noticed something— something desperate in the man's deep-set eyes, something sad and lonesome. Had he never seen it before? Had he never cared?

Eric knew he had changed since his father's death, but he was still trying to figure out how. There was indeed a big hole in his life, and he would always miss his dad. Yes, life would never be what it once was, but maybe he now had the ability to see what he had never seen before—the needs, torments, and loneliness of others. Instead of trying to push away all his emotions, maybe the answer was to let God use them to help others. To speak up for the poor and the helpless. To defend those who aren't able to help themselves.

Eric walked back to the homeless man, offered his hand to him, and lifted him up off the sidewalk. He bought him a meal at a local café, and he let the man tell him his life story. Eric shared his faith in Christ and then helped the man to a nearby shelter.

Eric discovered that God could make good come from great loss. He could redeem the cruelest pain and the deepest sorrow. He could use his new tenderness of the soul—and in the helping could come healing.

Lord, please turn my sadness into compassion that I might be a help to others who are in great need. Amen.

GOD'S GREAT FAITHFULNESS

Your faithfulness extends to every generation,
like the earth you created; it endures by your
decree, for everything serves your plans.
PSALM 119:90–91 TLB

*A*s Glenn moved through the passages of grief over the loss of his only child, he learned one thing—that people sometimes fail you when you need them the most. And there seemed to be a hundred reasons why. Some people simply have few friendship skills. Or maybe they know how to be a friend when times are good—when everyone is laughing and kicking back to watch a game—but not so much when you're in a joyless place of heartache. Or perhaps some friends aren't good with words, and they don't know what to say when tragedy strikes. Or they don't like hanging out if they think death will be the main topic of conversation. Then there are the friends who make too many demands too soon when you're mourning. Too bad that when you're finally ready to get out into the fresh air or go out to eat, there is no one left to connect with. They are all too frustrated or offended. "Oh, how complicated and unsteady and hypersensitive we are, Lord," Glenn prayed. "Me included."

But over time, Glenn learned a more important truth—that while people may sometimes fail, God does not fail. His faithfulness extends to every generation, every heart. God is solid. He is trustworthy. He is there. And He has a plan.

Almighty God, even when the whole world seems to flee from me in my time of need, I choose to trust in You. I praise You and thank You for Your faithfulness. Please show me Your divine plan, and give me the strength to pursue it. In Jesus' name I pray. Amen.

FINDING A GOOD DAY

———————◆———————

*Turn to me [LORD] and be gracious to me, for I am
alone and afflicted. The troubles of my heart are
multiplied; bring me out of my distresses.*
PSALM 25:16–17 AMP

*W*illow had a good day—but there hadn't
been a lot of good days since her mom died. To
Willow, sometimes her life seemed like a strange
board game. When it came to mourning her
mother's death, she'd take one step forward by
having a happy moment, and then suddenly a
wave of grief would hit her, forcing her back ten
steps.

Willow never knew when the waves would
hit her. One painful surge might come out of a
pleasant memory or something humorous her
mother used to do or say. It might come from a
gesture that she found herself making that looked
just like her mom's. Or if Willow wanted to call
her mom about a problem, she'd suddenly and
sadly remember that calling was no longer possible. All the calling and laughing and lunching
and shopping and heart-sharing days were over.

She could no longer ask her mom questions about the future. She couldn't tell her about her dates or the progress in her career or get her advice on marriage. Even amid the sadness, though, Willow wanted to learn how to accept her loss. But what did God expect her to do with all the remembering days? The "I miss you more than words can say" days? Willow wondered if God could help her reach a point when the remembering days would bring her a smile of love instead of a heart full of pain. Willow prayed for that very miracle.

Lord, please help me remember the past
with more smiles than sorrow. Amen.

WONDROUS JOY

"It will be the same joy as that of a woman in labor when her child is born—her anguish gives place to rapturous joy and the pain is forgotten. You have sorrow now, but I will see you again and then you will rejoice; and no one can rob you of that joy."
JOHN 16:21–22 TLB

*M*ankind was made for joy—made to delight in God and all His many gifts—and yet after the death of a loved one, we can't help but wonder, *Will I ever be happy again? Would the joy be attached to guilt? Or would my choice of joy represent a reliance on the Savior?*

The death of Kendra's two brothers in a car accident caused a cold sadness to settle in her soul. But one day in the garden, she noticed an unlikely sight. A patch of daffodils had pushed their way up through the spring snow and burst into bloom. Kendra smiled. The orange and yellow petals—still sprinkled with icy crystals—got hit with a sunbeam, and the glorious radiance of the blooms was enough to make anyone's heart warm. How could something so fresh and glowing and beautiful really come out of something so cold and frosty?

Kendra pushed through her sorrow and chose to see what was still possible and what was still beautiful in the world. She thought, *Just as no one can rob me of the joy of being a Christian and knowing I will one day meet my Savior face-to-face, I also know that no one can take away this divine moment of healing and happiness.* She prayed there would be more moments of wondrous joy—many more.

Lord, I need Your divine joy again. Amen.

HIS PERFECT WAY

*For it is you who light my lamp; the LORD
my God lightens my darkness. For by you I
can run against a troop, and by my God I can
leap over a wall. This God—his way is perfect;
the word of the LORD proves true; he is a shield
for all those who take refuge in him.*

PSALM 18:28–30 ESV

*B*lended families can be like a glorious mosaic
made of many wonderful pieces, but when met
with a family death, that beautiful family picture
can become damaged. Family members may
come together with unique backgrounds or
expectations, and they may grieve differently.
Each one may be hurt, confused, or angry over
the way the funeral was handled or the way the
inheritance was divided, or they may suffer from
any number of familial changes that happen during the bereavement. Strong emotions may rise
and threaten to destroy even the most stable
relationships. How can a family deal with such an
onslaught?

All families need tremendous patience, com-
mitment, and love. Talking the problems through

and listening with an open heart is a good start. Going to a Bible-based counselor is another option. But all families need prayer. As we humble ourselves before God, He will meet with us in our pain, and He promises to change our world. Prayer might give the illusion that not much is happening, and yet prayers are powerful. The Bible says, "Therefore, confess your sins to one another and pray for one another, that you may be healed. The prayer of a righteous person has great power as it is working" (James 5:16 ESV).

So, when a beautiful blended family, or any family, is in need of direction—seek the Lord's way, for it is perfect.

---

*Lord, please guide our family as we try
to love our way through our loss. Amen.*

WALKING HUMBLY

———— •••• ————

He has told you, O mortal, what is good; and what
does the LORD require of you but to do justice, and to
love kindness, and to walk humbly with your God?
MICAH 6:8 NRSV

What would life look like if we truly walked humbly with God? Peaceful? Loving? Full of divine light? It would be true life like no other. But what happens when that beautiful, intimate, and humble walk with God gets interrupted with the tragic loss of our beloved? The peace may get shattered—like a plate-glass window, with shards scattering everything, cutting us as well as wounding anyone who comes near to the brokenness. Because of the rebellion in the Garden of Eden, we live in a perilous world. Christ came to offer us redemption, power over sin, and eternal life, but until we go to heaven or until Christ's Second Coming, we Christians still reside on this broken earth.

So, how are we to live with death and loneliness? In the book of Job we are reminded, "Then his wife said to him, 'Do you still persist in your integrity? Curse God, and die.' But he said to her, 'You speak as any foolish woman would speak. Shall we receive the good at the hand of God, and not receive the bad?' In all this Job did not sin with his lips" (Job 2:9–10 NRSV).

Yes, in the good and even in the bad things that come to us, we can do what is right. We can still love kindness and justice. We can still walk humbly with our Lord. There is no walk more beautiful.

Lord, I have seen triumphs in this life, and I have known great trials. No matter the circumstances, I choose to walk with You by my side. Amen.

A TABLE FOR ONE

―――――•―――――

*"No one has greater love [nor stronger commitment]
than to lay down his own life for his friends. You are
my friends if you keep on doing what I command you.
I do not call you servants any longer, for the servant
does not know what his master is doing; but I have
called you [My] friends, because I have revealed to you
everything that I have heard from My Father."*
JOHN 15:13–15 AMP

*B*ridget sat in the lovely French restaurant by
herself. It had always been her favorite. But the
empty seat across from her bothered her. "Table
for one" were the words she'd said to the hostess
who seated her. The waiters then removed all the
extra dishes, stemware, and silverware. By the
time the "removal" production was over, Bridget
wished she hadn't even bothered to eat out.

But then one moment later, her gal friend
showed up after all, even though she didn't think
she'd be able to come. Bridget almost burst into
tears of joy when she saw her friend. The delight-
ful surprise was glorious and so very welcome.
At that moment, Bridget realized how friendship

deprived she had been. And how much she needed to keep reaching out to friends, not just for social occasions, but for encouragement, laughter, comradery, and prayers. Bridget breathed a prayer, "Thank You, God, for this special surprise tonight and for the gift of friendship."

Then Bridget remembered the scripture that talked about the friendship of Christ. Bridget prayed again, "Lord, You are my dearest friend. Always. Please be our special guest this evening."

Lord, as I surround myself with good and godly friends, I want You to know that You will always be my very best friend! Amen.

THE WEIGHT OF GLORY

———◆———

*So we do not lose heart. Though our outer
self is wasting away, our inner self is being
renewed day by day. For this light momentary
affliction is preparing for us an eternal weight
of glory beyond all comparison, as we look
not to the things that are seen but to the things
that are unseen. For the things that are seen are
transient, but the things that are unseen are eternal.*

2 CORINTHIANS 4:16–18 ESV

As the years passed, Jeremy had accepted the
loss of his two uncles, but now the sudden passing
of his favorite nephew was hard to bear. So vibrant
and so full of youthful and noble dreams. At times
Jeremy sat in his small library and pondered life
and death. When his thoughts were tempted to
head into too many hopeless directions, he'd pick
up his Bible. Sometimes it would fall open to
just the passage he needed. Today 2 Corinthians
reminded him that while his outer shell was
wasting away, his inner self was being renewed.
He was reminded that the afflictions of this life
were not going to last forever, and that the weight

of glory that he would one day know in heaven would far surpass all the troubles and tears and death in this fallen and fleeting realm. Yes, when Jeremy felt himself leaning toward despair in the future, he would remind himself not to stay so intensely focused on the temporary visible world before him—but to keep his hope in what is eternal and glorious in God's unseen world.

Lord, I trust You with my past, my present, and my future. Remind me daily how temporary this life is and that my hope should be in You and Your promise of eternal life. Amen.

BE MINE FOREVER!

———— ◆ ————

My health fails; my spirits droop, yet God remains!
He is the strength of my heart; he is mine forever!
PSALM 73:26 TLB

There will be times when you may forget the sustaining power of God. It might come from the death of your best friend. And this passing of a loved one might be compounded by other trials, such as a long series of disappointments, a betrayal, a debilitating illness, financial ruin, or chronic depression.

Whatever you are facing, remember the past. How did God sustain you in bygone times? It is good to remember and to write down all that God has done for you throughout your life so that when the days and hours of living seem impossible, or it feels as though you aren't really living at all but merely existing, you will be lifted up. When the world offers no real truth—remember, your life has not been a series of random events but a lacing together of miracles like the finest string of heavenly pearls.

When we open our eyes to God's truth, we

can clearly see that His sustaining and redemptive power can be witnessed in all things great and small throughout our lives. We are reminded in Psalms that when one's health fails and one's spirit droops, yet God will remain. When the rest of the world falls away, the Lord will be trustworthy and true. What hope! Yes, let God be our mighty strength. May we say to the Lord, "I remember the past and Your sustaining power. I am thankful for Your grace and mercy. Be mine forever!"

Lord, I choose to remember all that You've done for me in the past, and I will put my trust in You as we face the future together. Amen.

A WALK IN THE WOODS

"Peace I leave with you; My [perfect] peace I give to you; not as the world gives do I give to you. Do not let your heart be troubled, nor let it be afraid. [Let My perfect peace calm you in every circumstance and give you courage and strength for every challenge.]"
JOHN 14:27 AMP

*P*erry drove out to the country, trying to get away from the busy crowds and noise of the city. He needed a long walk in the woods. That was always where he'd found his peace before—because it was a place where he liked to meet with God. So, he parked and headed out on his favorite trail, trying to process the shock and confusion of his current situation—that is, the death of his business partner.

The man's friendship would be greatly missed, and his honest and hardworking approach to business would be hard to replace. What a loss for everyone. What a shock. The more Perry tried to understand all the whys, the more questions that arose. Finally, Perry sat down on a tree stump, clasped his hands, and said to the Lord, "Why,

God, did he have to die? I don't understand. Perhaps I never will. What will happen now?"

Then Perry recalled John 14:27—a verse he'd memorized in his youth. He repeated it out loud. Once again, he took the words from his head down to his heart, and he stayed right there on that stump, connecting to the only real peace that this world will ever know—Jesus Christ.

Lord God, thank You for the promise of peace, even in the midst of life's worst trials. I am trusting You for Your supernatural courage and strength to get me through. Amen.

HE HAS GIVEN US HIS WORD

———————•———————

*All Scripture is breathed out by God and profitable
for teaching, for reproof, for correction, and for
training in righteousness, that the man of God
may be complete, equipped for every good work.*
2 TIMOTHY 3:16–17 ESV

*S*ometimes we need a word from God. Even
on an ordinary day, we need God. Nothing and
no one else will do. And when we face the tragic
loss of a loved one, we can get frantic wanting to
know if God is still there for us, still loving us.
You might think, *I wish God would write His words
out for me each morning. Wouldn't it be wonderful
to see those divine words gilded in gold and even
sending off sacred sparks of lightning as they swirl
before me?*

We might not see any physical manifestations
of fire or lightning, but God does give us His
guidance anytime we choose to see it. God calls it
the Bible, and all the scripture within its pages is
breathed out by Him. This living Book speaks to
us anew every day through the power of the Holy
Spirit. It is not a dusty, ancient tome to be stored

up high on a library shelf, but a magnificent living document full of the fiery fervor of a God who loved mankind enough to send His Son to taste death for us and to make sure that we through Christ could have victory over it. When we embrace that glorious grace of Christ's sacrifice on the cross and His forgiveness of sins, then that dark abyss of death becomes flooded with the eternal light and life of Christ.

Yes, we serve that kind of good God, and He is always here for us. He has given us His Word.

Lord, please show me the way not only during my times of prayer but when I read Your Holy Word! Amen.

HOPE

May the God of hope fill you with all joy and peace in believing [through the experience of your faith] that by the power of the Holy Spirit you will abound in hope and overflow with confidence in His promises.

Romans 15:13 AMP

*H*umanity longs for *hope*. Such a small word, but it holds such a bold and beautiful meaning! Without it, nothing else matters. We can try, but what earthly pleasure could we possibly cook up to make us happy if we had no hope in our today or our tomorrows? Or in our eternity? Humans need hope to survive—to enjoy life, to laugh, to work, to play, and to love. Not the hope the world offers, but the real deal.

After the rebellion in the Garden, the earth fell into spiritual ruin, no longer the perfect sanctuary of love and light that we were meant to enjoy. But even in our rebellion, even in our sinful condition, God has given us hope through Jesus Christ. We can have victory now and the hope of heaven in the future. And if that wasn't wonderful enough, before Jesus' death and resurrection, He promised to leave us with a Comforter—the Holy Spirit. The book of Romans tells us, "May the God of hope fill you with all joy and peace in believing [through the experience of your faith] that by the power of the Holy Spirit you will abound in hope and overflow with confidence in His promises."

Even when the world or the enemy of your soul tries to destroy you with every manner of temptation and sorrow, misery and illness, and even when you may suffer the loss of your beloved, hope is here. Comfort is real. The promise still holds.

Lord, thank You for Your glorious hope! Amen.

DRENCHED IN LOVE

I'm asking GOD for one thing, only one thing:
To live with him in his house my whole life long.
I'll contemplate his beauty; I'll study at his feet.
That's the only quiet, secure place in a noisy world,
the perfect getaway, far from the buzz of traffic.
PSALM 27:4–5 MSG

This world is a noisy, busy, clamoring place. So much so, it's hard to find a refuge. And it may be harder still when you're dealing with the death of a dear friend or a beloved member of your family.

When you do find a special spot of sanctuary, what is it you long for most? Isn't it to know that God is still with you? To know that He sees your tears and hears your sighs and your shouts? That His love and care for you have never diminished throughout all your sufferings? And don't you long to be in God's divine presence? Perhaps it could happen bobbing on a boat out on a silvery pond. Or up on the summit of a snow-laden mountain. Or while strolling through a meadow just coming into bloom. Ah yes. Refuge with Him. . .

But when you can't get away, you can meet

with the Lord right where you are, even if it's in the middle of a traffic jam. Or in the middle of the messiest mayhem the world has to offer. Because wherever you are, God is there. He can create peace-filled getaways for the soul. He can encircle you in His mighty arms. There you may contemplate His beauty. You may study at His feet and gain wisdom about the future. Time with the Lord is never wasted—it is time spent drenched in love.

Wherever I am, Lord,
please be present in my life. Amen.

GOD HAS A PLAN

———————— ◆ ————————

"For I know the plans I have for you," declares the LORD, "plans to prosper you and not to harm you, plans to give you hope and a future."
JEREMIAH 29:11 NIV

Many months had passed since the death of Kendall's wife, and even though he was trying to accept his extraordinary loss—and even though he'd known joy playing with his grandkids—he still worried about his future. Kendall sometimes thought, *I don't know what to do next. Does God still have a plan for me in my retirement years? I wake up in the morning staring at the ceiling, and my friends keep saying that if I wake up breathing, then God has a reason for it and a purpose for my life.* But Kendall had to admit that sometimes his friends' speeches came off a little artificial and canned. Or they seemed like mini lectures to jostle him into living again. Kendall still missed his wife. He missed the hugs, the smiles, and the longs walks in the evening. The way her hand slipped so easily into his as they strolled along. Kendall told a friend, "I see now that there will never come a time that I won't pine for her. But I do know too that I needed that jostling." One morning, Kendall said to God, "I do feel like You have a hope and future for me, Lord. What is it? Could You show me Your plan? I am not sure I feel emotionally ready, but in Your strength, I am willing to lean on You as we walk into the future together."

---

*Lord, I know You love me and You
have a divine plan. Please show me
the way. Every day. Every hour. Amen.*

IN SEARCH OF JOY

Those who sow with tears will reap with songs of joy.
Those who go out weeping, carrying seed to sow, will
return with songs of joy, carrying sheaves with them.
PSALM 126:5–6 NIV

*H*ave you ever been in search of joy? It may be closer than you think.

Chloe—who's frail father had passed away months earlier in a nursing home—sat sad and silent on her front porch swing. But in the next moment, the sun broke loose from a cloud, and a robin hopped up on the porch railing. The bird released a soprano-like trill—a sweet song of joy. Chloe sat very still as the robin cocked its head at her, this way and that, and then flitted off on its way.

A neighbor dropped by to visit, and Chloe told her, "I saw a robin just now, and my heart lurched. I think it was joy. Didn't see it coming, the bird or the joy." They both smiled. "But it pleased me." For a moment, in that tiniest of wonders, Chloe saw that such a creative God could be bigger than her pain. Greater than her fears. Chloe saw a thing of delight and heard a song of joy, and she embraced it in her heart.

Sometimes encouragement comes in the big sweeping turns of life, and sometimes it arrives in a small wisp of a thing—like a robin full of song and pausing to be curious about you.

Psalm 94:19 (AMP) says, "When my anxious thoughts multiply within me, Your comforts delight me."

What would bring you joy and delight today?

Lord, I need some joy in my life. May we go in search of it today—together. Amen.

POWERFUL MEDICINE

Whoever is kind to the poor lends to the LORD,
and he will reward them for what they have done.
PROVERBS 19:17 NIV

When you're trying to cope with grief that comes from the loss of a loved one, it is hard to focus on anything else but your current emotions. You may choose to stay in a cocoon-like mode for a while, and that may be just where the Lord wants you to be. To rest and refresh with Him by your side. Perhaps with a few loyal friends who can come alongside you. Then, in between the dark and surging waves of grief, you might suddenly get a glimpse of the sun glistening on the horizon.

One man in mourning said, "The local food pantry sign that read, 'In Need of Extra Supplies' had been there a long time as I drove past it on my way to work, but I had never really payed much attention to it. I began to wonder how it would feel to be truly hungry and needy. I suddenly wanted to help."

Sometimes in the various passages of bereavement, we may gain the ability to see and feel the suffering of others more keenly. Empathy is powerful medicine when it comes to the healing of others, and God can use that powerful medicine.

Romans 8:28 (esv) tells us, "And we know that for those who love God all things work together for good, for those who are called according to his purpose."

Since God is in the business of redemption, ask Him what can come from your great loss. Where can He use this powerful healing medicine of empathy?

Lord, please use me to help others in pain.
Show me what I can do. Amen.

BITS OF GLADNESS

———— ● ————

When God's children are in need, you be
the one to help them out. And get into the
habit of inviting guests home for dinner or,
if they need lodging, for the night.
ROMANS 12:13 TLB

*A*lice sat in her office chair, twiddling her pen. She did a lot of that lately. Not really working. Just twiddling. She couldn't focus well on the tasks at hand, let alone organize her work for the months ahead. She did stay at work late though, to make up for all the drifting and, well, twiddling. It was easy to stay late since going home and eating alone and watching TV alone was challenging to say the least.

Her husband had passed away some months earlier, and the solitude was slowly eating away at her. Alice prayed, "Lord, I miss my husband. I'm not sure what to do. I need company. The church said they needed people to host various events in their homes, like Bible studies, ladies' luncheons, and dinners for visiting missionaries.

Perhaps this would be a way to let go of some of the relentless solitude. I could start small and see if I could handle the strain of a few people coming and going. Lord, maybe You want this to be a way to bless all of us."

Alice gave hospitality a try. The events took some time, some effort, and some patience, but the terrible lonesomeness Alice had felt lifted some. Little by little, Alice came to see seeds of gladness budding and then flourishing in her heart as she brought joy to others.

Lord, I am sad, but I sense You want to give me a holy resilience. Perhaps You would like me to reach out to others. Show me how to offer the gift of hospitality. Amen.

THE LOVE OF GOD

*For I am sure that neither death nor life, nor angels
nor rulers, nor things present nor things to come,
nor powers, nor height nor depth, nor anything
else in all creation, will be able to separate us
from the love of God in Christ Jesus our Lord.*
ROMANS 8:38–39 ESV

*T*he couple had always adored their child—
Brianna. When she was born, the couple believed
that the sun had surely shined a little brighter that
day and the flowers had smelled a little sweeter.
She was their darling in every way. So, when the
time came for her fifth birthday party, Brianna's
parents couldn't help but give her a glorious day.
There was a crowd of family and friends to help
the little girl celebrate. Lots of food and laughter.
A big gooey cake with candles aglow. Treats for
Brianna's friends and so many gifts that she couldn't
keep track of them all. There was even a neighbor dressed up as her favorite movie character.
People looked on at the spectacle, smiled, and said,
"Yeah, they are over the moon about their child."

If we fallible humans can love our kids so

enthusiastically—and even surprise them with more gifts than they can keep track of—then wouldn't our Father in heaven love us even more than that? After all, God is the Creator of love.

If you haven't thought of that divine truth lately, ponder it and hold on to it. Delight in the fact that God not only loves and cares for you, but He is utterly over the moon about you.

Lord, thank You for loving me through every victory and every sorrow and for giving me so many good gifts. I love You too! Amen.

A JOYFUL MIND

*A happy heart is good medicine and
a joyful mind causes healing, but a
broken spirit dries up the bones.*
PROVERBS 17:22 AMP

*E*mily was born with what people called a bright and breezy temperament, and she had always relished a good, hearty laugh. But when her mother died and then her aunt and uncle, it felt as though her life had closed down like the final curtain in a theater. The smiles and laughter left her and became no more than a distant memory. Emily felt as though her very bones had dried up as it mentions in Proverbs.

Emily had always been that jovial encouragement when others needed a happy heart, but now she needed help, and she didn't like being on the needy end of things. It made her feel awkward and uncomfortably vulnerable. And yet Emily reached out anyway, humbling herself and sharing her life with genuine openness. And in that frailness and genuineness, Emily received a new friend—someone who made *her* laugh and allowed her to see life anew.

Month by month, Emily gradually felt a lightening in her spirit. She had trusted in the Lord, even in the hardest of days, and He had been faithful to help her and comfort her, but He had also provided her with that earthly friend—a true serendipity. Emily's friend helped her see that having a sunny disposition again didn't mean that she had loved her family less. It simply meant trusting God. That even in the midst of missing those you love, it was also possible to have a joyful mind and a merry heart.

Lord, even though I will always miss my loved ones, thank You for Your comfort, for the beauty of friendship, and the merry moments of healing. Amen.

PEACH PIE

———◆———

You make known to me the path of life;
in your presence there is fullness of joy;
at your right hand are pleasures forevermore.
PSALM 16:11 ESV

*N*oah had always loved peach pie. When he was a kid—and the peach tree in the backyard was ripe with the fruit—he'd be the first one to fill a small basket and take it to his mom. Then came the transformation from peaches to home-made pie. And oh, the cinnamon smell of it and that first sweet bite. Nothing else like it. Such memories were welcome—until his mom died. Noah realized that the pie didn't mean much without the maker of that confection.

So, when an elderly neighbor had dropped off a peach pie, he'd thanked her kindly, closed the door, and stared at the pie with some suspicion. "Hmmm. How did the woman know it was my favorite?" It felt warm like it was right out of the oven. The aroma wafting off the pie almost smelled good. Before he could talk himself out of it, Noah took a small slice out onto the front porch and took a bite. Oh, the neighbor did indeed have the gift of pie making. Memories came trickling back. He recalled that in his youth his mother would sometimes help him make a separate smaller pie just for fun. Yes, there was a piercing of the heart with the memories, but there was also a measure of joy in knowing that his mother had loved her family enough to provide them with not only great food but many wonderful recollections.

Noah took another bite. Yes, there was a lot going on in that simple gift of peach pie.

Lord, thank You for the simple joys You send me. Sometimes they make all the difference. Amen.

BE FILLED WITH JOY!

"When you obey me you are living in my love,
just as I obey my Father and live in his love.
I have told you this so that you will be filled
with my joy. Yes, your cup of joy will overflow!"
JOHN 15:10–11 TLB

*H*ave you ever had a fountain drink accidentally overflow and then spill all over the floor? It can create quite the sticky mess. But if we had good things overflow in our lives, oh, how welcome and wonderful that would be! We all need some wonderful in our lives, especially when we've experienced the hardship of loss. Because God is full of love and His heart is set on redemption, He is in the business of wonderful. He can provide us with what is marvelous, delight filled, and even breathtaking. We can overflow with joy.

After the loss of a loved one, we might think that our gladness has all dried up and that we will never feel the abundance of it again. But the Word of God tells us to obey the Lord's precepts, and when we do that, we'll be living in the love of Christ.

May we always love the Lord in return, not with the leftover dregs of our affections after we've poured our love out to everything else, but as a firstfruit of the vine offering to the One who loves us beyond our wildest imaginings. And in that mutual love, may we rest in the elegant beauty of His light and the wonderful fellowship of His presence.

Dearest Lord Jesus, I want to know joy. Please help me be obedient, not out of obligation, but from a grateful heart. And help me love You as You have loved me. Amen.

MY FATHER'S WORK

*Everyone was surprised and impressed that a
12-year-old boy could have such deep understanding
and could answer questions with such wisdom.
His parents, of course, had a different reaction.*
Mary: *Son, why have You treated us this way?
Listen, Your father and I have been sick with
worry for the last three days, wondering where
You were, looking everywhere for You.*
Jesus: *Why did you need to look for Me? Didn't
you know that I must be working for My Father?*
LUKE 2:47–49 VOICE

God gives us a purpose in this life. Otherwise, we
would feel rather aimless and empty. People need
purpose to thrive. Jesus came with a holy mission,
and He fulfilled it—lovingly, supernaturally, and
perfectly.

The enemy may tell you that your purpose is
trifling, but if God has given it to you, it is real and
it is vital. After the loss of a loved one though, life
is indeed altered—and yet in the midst of sorrow,
we can still have purpose.

What has God given you to do? If the idea

of a noble calling or an ambitious list of tasks seems overwhelming at the moment, maybe you could take it one step at a time. What is one thing you could do to help someone this week? Is there someone you know who is hurting in the same way you are hurting? Could you offer a word of compassion, a freshly baked casserole, or a listening ear? Sometimes the simplest gift of kindness can have a huge and life-changing impact.

Father God, I am in need of a purpose.
I want to do Your will and be the salt and
light of this world. Help me, because I can't
do this alone. In Jesus' name I pray. Amen.

THE GOD WHO PURSUES ME

———— ◆ ————

Is there anyplace I can go to avoid your Spirit?
to be out of your sight? If I climb to the sky, you're
there! If I go underground, you're there! If I flew on
morning's wings to the far western horizon, You'd
find me in a minute—you're already there waiting!
Then I said to myself, "Oh, he even sees me in the
dark! At night I'm immersed in the light!" It's a fact:
darkness isn't dark to you; night and day, darkness
and light, they're all the same to you.
PSALM 139:7–12 MSG

*W*hen life turns tragic, when life oppresses, or
when life offers us nothing but solitude, we need
to know that God is still there. That He will still
draw near to us—understanding us, loving us,
and caring for us through it all. Even when we
collapse in fear and hopelessness, trying to make
sense of our tragedy, He is there. When we try
to run away or hide, God is there. The Lord goes
beyond waiting for us; He will pursue us. There
is no escape from His love. Even on the blackest
day and in the darkest hour, the Lord is right there,
pursuing you as the Lover of your soul—you are

the apple of His eye. This glorious love is hard to fathom, and yet, oh so very welcome!

Father God, I can sense that You are ever in pursuit of me. I am relieved and happy to know this facet of Your divine character. I thank You and praise You for Your tender mercies, for Your everlasting love, and for not giving up on me! In Jesus' holy name I pray. Amen.

GREAT AND HIDDEN THINGS

———————•———————

*"Call to me and I will answer you,
and will tell you great and hidden
things that you have not known."*

JEREMIAH 33:3 ESV

*Y*our best friend meets you for lunch, and after an hour of chitchatting, she suddenly takes on a more somber look as she slowly sets her napkin down. You know your friend well enough to guess that she is about to tell you some personal secret. Something she will tell only you—her very dearest friend. Why? Because she trusts you with the stories of her heart. She knows that you have proven yourself to be well-intentioned and wise with these hidden things. Perhaps the secret is her deepest fear. Perhaps it is about a financial worry that she needs you to pray about. Maybe the news is concerning a bad medical report, and she's scared. Perhaps the information is lighter in nature, and she wants to tell you that she is pregnant, and she wants you to celebrate with her!

When we read this verse in Jeremiah 33:3, we can't help but be in awe over what the Lord might share with us in His presence. After all, He loves us and considers us His dearest friends. This reminder in Jeremiah isn't just for ancient prophets, but for modern-day Christians as well. Approach the Lord with reverence, repentance, requests, and thanksgiving and praise. Then wait patiently and quietly on the Lord with sweet expectation. The Lord may surprise you with great and hidden things from His heart.

Father God, I love You, and I want to get to know You better. Teach me how to be still and bask in Your holy and enlightening presence. In Jesus' name I pray. Amen.

A LIVING HOPE

———•———

*Blessed be the God and Father of our Lord
Jesus Christ! According to his great mercy, he has
caused us to be born again to a living hope through
the resurrection of Jesus Christ from the dead,
to an inheritance that is imperishable, undefiled,
and unfading, kept in heaven for you.*

1 PETER 1:3–4 ESV

*P*eople hate the idea of dying. When we are surrounded by life, it is indeed a hard concept to ponder. But what if someone gave you a magical elixir to drink—a potion that would give you immortality on this earth? Would you take it? Remember, the elixir doesn't change your heart or the condition of the earth and its peoples—it only changes the fact that you will be left in your body as it is for all time. Is that really what we crave? After deeper consideration, absolutely not! So, you throw the bottle down on the pavement and watch the glass as it shatters into bits and as the liquid curls its way down the sewer drain.

That is the only sane response. Who would want to live forever inside our frail bodies?

Suffering forever from chronic illnesses, accidents, and maladies of the mind? Enduring torments from earthly strife, spiritual oppression, wars, famine, and natural disasters? Yes, what would at first seem like a miracle in a bottle would soon become a curse.

As Christians we live with the greatest hope there is—eternal life in heaven with our Lord. It doesn't get any better than that. May we cling to that hope and find daily comfort in that promise.

Heavenly Father, I am so grateful You didn't leave us here in our sins but made a way for our redemption. Thank You for this glorious inheritance. I am so very grateful! In Jesus' name I pray. Amen.

A TIME FOR MENDING

*"So if you are offering your gift at the altar and
there remember that your brother has something
against you, leave your gift there before the altar
and go. First be reconciled to your brother,
and then come and offer your gift."*
MATTHEW 5:23–24 ESV

*E*ven when life is going pretty smoothly, and
we're putting our best foot forward, it's hard to
say all the right things and do all the right things.
Sometimes feelings can get hurt easily with family,
friends, coworkers, and church folks. Even if you
managed to say the perfect words, what you
say still might be offensive because people are
looking at life from different perspectives. They
are coming at the conversation with different
backgrounds and experiences—and that is true
even for two children who've been raised in the
same household. So, if you add the death of a
loved one to that complicated mix, there's bound
to be some trouble. People might have gotten
their feelings hurt because you were too exhausted
emotionally to call them back after the funeral, or

you said some things in anger because you were at the height of your grief.

After some time has passed and you feel yourself gaining some strength, it would be good to ask the Lord about the situation. Is there someone you need to contact for reconciliation? Now is always a good time for forgiveness, for mending, for healing. It will be cleansing to the soul—not to mention how it will make God smile—and it will bring refreshment and joy to all concerned. And joy is something we all need more of.

Lord, please show me the people who I need to go to and reconcile with. I want my life to feel the refreshment of forgiveness. Please give me the courage to follow through. Amen.

THE FACE OF KINDNESS

As God's chosen ones, holy and beloved, clothe yourselves with compassion, kindness, humility, meekness, and patience.

Colossians 3:12 nrsv

Try to remember the various times in your life when a simple act of kindness brought you comfort and joy. Some of those episodes may stand out as surprising, remarkable, and maybe even life-changing. Were those moments so heartwarming that they made you want to pass it on? Perhaps you were inspired enough to want to go out and offer someone else a similar gift of kindness.

You don't need a big bank account to offer bits of benevolence as you go through your days. Kindness might come in the form of offering patience in a difficult situation or allowing a harried mom to go in front of you in the line at the grocery store. Perhaps it is a few words of encouragement when someone is in dire need of reassurance, or words of praise for a job well done. Maybe it's no more than a smile in a sea of frowns, or a batch of freshly baked cookies.

Or maybe it is offering a listening ear to people who have known loss and grief—just as you have. The empathy that you can bring to the situation could be healing and life-changing for them.

Perhaps this is a good time to ask the Lord for opportunities to shine for Him. To reach out to others in their many distresses. To be that beautiful face of kindness that the whole world is longing and needing to see.

―――――――――――――――――――――

Dear God, I want to reach out to others who might need a cup of compassion. Perhaps I could even help those who have gone through the same grief that I have known. Please guide me in this holy endeavor. In Jesus' name I pray. Amen.

WHAT WILL THE
FUTURE HOLD?

---

*And my God will fully satisfy every need of yours
according to his riches in glory in Christ Jesus.*
PHILIPPIANS 4:19 NRSV

*E*ven when life brings some measure of joy
again, you may always feel sadness over the passing of your loved one or a longing for the way
life once was. But even then, the Lord may have
some things He wants you to accomplish. Moving
forward in faith doesn't mean you would be
forgetting your beloved, nor would it diminish
his or her memory in any way.

Along with that willingness to fulfill your
divine purpose, perhaps honest questions will
still linger. God is big; He can handle questions.
"What will my life look like in the future? Is it a
good time to start a new career? To sell the house?
Will my financial needs be met? How will I cope
with all the loneliness as the years drift by? Who
will take care of me if I become ill?" There will
continue to be questions throughout our lives, no

matter our situation, but the Bible says, "And my God will fully satisfy every need of yours according to his riches in glory in Christ Jesus."

The Bible also encourages us by saying, "He gives strength to the weary, and to him who has no might He increases power" (Isaiah 40:29 AMP).

These are promises offered by the One who has the authority to offer them. The Lord is faithful to take care of His people, and when the time is right, He will love His people right through those heavenly gates.

Lord, I want to trust You fully with my future. May we move forward together, and may I embrace my future with hope and joy. Amen.

A SENSE OF AWE

O LORD, how manifold are your works! In wisdom have you made them all; the earth is full of your creatures. Here is the sea, great and wide, which teems with creatures innumerable, living things both small and great. There go the ships, and Leviathan, which you formed to play in it.
PSALM 104:24–26 ESV

We reside in a world intertwined with many blessings and many burdens—and sometimes we are either too busy or too riddled with pain to witness the wonder. In our suffering, may we not allow the enemy to keep us from seeing the beauty of the moment or the awe right before us. God supplies us with a million marvels to keep us occupied and hope-filled and teeming with curiosity and absolute delight.

Psalm 19:1 (ESV) reminds us, "The heavens declare the glory of God, and the sky above proclaims his handiwork." We can praise God for so many glories—the alpine mists swirling over the mountain peaks, waterfalls thundering down through the canyons, the night sky lit with celestial mystery, the vast world under the microscope, the oceans teeming with every kind of life imaginable—and some unfathomable. For even more delight, there are fire rainbows, frost flowers, fungus that glows, bugs that look like sticks, ice that looks like hair, frogs that sing like birds, birds that talk like people, and fish that fly like birds! We have so much to revel in—and so much yet to discover!

May we all get back to a place of awe. What is your list of favorite wonders? Is God wanting to show you some new ones?

Almighty Creator, help me not to miss all the wonders of this world. Bring me back to a place of awe in You and in Your glorious creation. In Jesus' name I pray. Amen.

WE HAVE A NOBLE CALLING

But the noble man conceives noble and
magnificent things; and he stands by
what is noble and magnificent.
ISAIAH 32:8 AMP

If you watch even a few minutes of the news, you will quickly discover that the world is having a nobility crisis. Yes, we have plenty of crowned heads, but what we are in short supply of is a sense of nobility—that is, morality, decency, and honorableness. There is at times such a scarcity of these virtues that we might get the idea that God has forsaken us. But the Lord is still very much with us, and He still wants to work through His people.

Matthew 5:14–16 (NIV) tells believers, "You are the light of the world. A town built on a hill cannot be hidden. Neither do people light a lamp and put it under a bowl. Instead they put it on its stand, and it gives light to everyone in the house. In the same way, let your light shine before others, that they may see your good deeds and glorify your Father in heaven."

What one simple thing would the Lord like you to do today that would be considered noble? Perhaps a selfless act or a kindness or taking up for someone who is helpless? What could you accomplish today? May we all conceive of magnificent things to do in the name of our Lord.

Holy Spirit, I want to use my time on this earth in a noble way. Please guide me in all I do. Even when I am struggling with the sorrows of my life, give me the strength and courage to fight for justice, to stand up for the voiceless, and to be a person of integrity, generosity, and compassion. Amen.

THIS GREAT HOPE

---

*"In my Father's house are many rooms. If it were not
so, would I have told you that I go to prepare a place
for you? And if I go and prepare a place for you, I will
come again and will take you to myself, that where I
am you may be also. And you know the way to where I
am going." Thomas said to him, "Lord, we do not know
where you are going. How can we know the way?"*
JOHN 14:2–5 ESV

*P*aula was ecstatic over her newly built dream
home in the country. The house had taken two
years to design, a year to build, and six months
to decorate. Paula and her husband even had a
special nursery created for the special times when
their grandbabies came to visit. They spared no
expense. It was all as glorious as they imagined.

But no matter how resplendent a home can be
on this side of eternity, there can be no comparison
to the home Christ is preparing for His beloved,
His followers. Since we know that the earth is a
place of spectacular beauty, then heaven will surely
be beyond all our grandest expectations.

Sometimes when it feels as though death is

all around you, it is easy to become overwhelmed with the thought of your own death. If that happens, take hold of God's promises. Embrace the love and grace of Christ. Heaven is real. God's Word is true. Be uplifted by this great hope.

Almighty God, I am in awe of Your promise of eternal life through Christ. Forgive me for my sins. I humbly repent and accept Your invitation to heaven. When the fear of death overtakes me, I will cling to Your promise of eternal life. In Jesus' name I pray. Amen.

This devotional book, *Comfort for Times of Loss*, is meant to encourage women and men who have known the loss of a loved one. But if you feel you need further help, you might want to consider some good Christian-based counseling. If you need emergency help for your grieving, please do not hesitate to call a suicide prevention hotline.

"May the Lord bless and protect you;
may the Lord's face radiate with joy
because of you; may he be gracious to you,
show you his favor, and give you his peace."
NUMBERS 6:24–26 TLB

ABOUT THE AUTHOR

Bestselling and award-winning author **Anita Higman** has fifty books published. She's been a Barnes & Noble "Author of the Month" for Houston and has a BA in the combined fields of speech communication, psychology, and art. A few of Anita's favorite things are fairytale castles, steampunk clothes, traveling through Europe, exotic teas like orchid and heather, romantic movies, and laughing with her friends. Feel free to drop by Anita's website at www.anitahigman.com. She would love to hear from you!

SCRIPTURE INDEX